Better Homes and Gardens®

SHORTCUT MAIN DISHES

BETTER HOMES AND GARDENS® BOOKS

Editor Gerald M. Knox
Art Director Ernest Shelton
Managing Editor David A. Kirchner
Copy and Production Editors James D. Blume, Marsha Jahns, Mary Helen Schiltz, Carl Voss

Food and Nutrition Editor Nancy Byal
Department Head, Cook Books Sharyl Heiken
Associate Department Heads Sandra Granseth, Rosemary C. Hutchinson, Elizabeth Woolever
Senior Food Editors Julia Malloy, Marcia Stanley, Joyce Trollope
Associate Food Editors Barbara Atkins, Linda Foley, Linda Henry, Lynn Hoppe,
Jill Johnson, Mary Jo Plutt, Maureen Powers, Martha Schiel
Recipe Development Editor Marion Viall
Test Kitchen Director Sharon Stilwell
Test Kitchen Photo Studio Director Janet Pittman
Test Kitchen Home Economists Jean Brekke, Kay Cargill, Marilyn Cornelius, Jennifer Darling,
Maryellyn Krantz, Lynelle Munn, Dianna Nolin, Marge Steenson,
Cynthia Volcko

Associate Art Directors Linda Ford Vermie, Neoma Alt West, Randall Yontz
Assistant Art Directors Lynda Haupert, Harijs Priekulis, Tom Wegner
Senior Graphic Designers Mike Eagleton, Lyne Neymeyer, Stan Sams
Graphic Designers Mike Burns, Sally Cooper, Jack Murphy, Darla Whipple-Frain,
Brian Wignall, Kimberly Zarley

Vice President, Editorial Director Doris Eby
Executive Director, Editorial Services Duane L. Gregg

Senior Vice President, General Manager Fred Stines
Director of Publishing Robert B. Nelson
Vice President, Retail Marketing Jamie Martin
Vice President, Direct Marketing Arthur Heydendael

Shortcut Main Dishes
Editor Joyce Trollope
Copy and Production Editor Mary Helen Schiltz
Graphic Designer Lynda Haupert
Electronic Text Processor Donna Russell
Photographers Michael Jensen and Sean Fitzgerald
Food Stylists Suzanne Finley, Dianna Nolin, Janet Pittman, Maria Rolandelli
Contributing Editor Sandra Mosley

On the cover
Ham and Shrimp Creole (see recipe, page 20)

Our seal assures you that every recipe in *Shortcut Main Dishes* has been tested in the Better Homes and Gardens® Test Kitchen. This means that each recipe is practical and reliable, and meets our high standards of taste appeal.

We know that you're busier than *ever* these days . . . with little time to cook. However, you *can* prepare—and enjoy—delicious meals by using some simple shortcuts. The help you need to start saving time in the kitchen is right here in your hands.

Each recipe in this book comes with a timetable to help you plan your own cooking schedule. A quick glance at the recipe reveals just how much time to allow.

In this book you'll also find a variety of practical, time-trimming cooking techniques to get you out of the kitchen *fast*. Utilize ready-to-serve foods from the deli. Or assemble a one-dish skillet meal. Give yourself a head start by stashing an extra meal in your freezer. Or, call on your slow cooker, oven, microwave, broiler, or wok to simplify your cooking. These timesaving shortcuts all add up to give you more time for the things you really enjoy!

Contents

Fix-It-Fast Sandwiches

For impromptu picnics, patio lunches, or light suppers, our sandwiches are unbeatable—and so-o-o-o easy! No cooking. No mess. No fuss. Simply stop at the deli for the ingredients. Then assemble your sandwich choice and you've got a great-tasting meal. For speedy cleanup, use paper plates.

Family-Size Hero Sandwich

Family-Size Hero Sandwich

A giant sandwich for giant appetites!

1 **16-ounce loaf unsliced Vienna bread** *or*
    French bread (16 to 20 inches long)
    Mayonnaise *or* **salad dressing**
    Prepared mustard (optional)
    Butter *or* **margarine, softened**
2 **medium tomatoes**
    Lettuce leaves
1 **pint purchased coleslaw, drained**
8 **ounces sliced boiled ham** *or*
    sliced bologna
1 **pint purchased marinated cucumbers
    and onions, drained**
4 **ounces sliced salami** *or* **sliced pepperoni**

Cut bread in half horizontally with a serrated or sharp, thin-bladed knife. Using a fork, hollow out center of bottom half of bread; leave a ½-inch-thick shell (see photo 1). Hollow out top of bread, if desired. Spread cut side of top half of bread with mayonnaise or salad dressing and mustard, if desired. Spread cut side of bottom half with butter or margarine.

Cut tomatoes into thin slices (see photo 2). Arrange lettuce over bottom half of loaf. Layer drained coleslaw, ham or bologna, tomato, drained cucumbers and onions, and salami or pepperoni over lettuce (see photo 3). Place top half of bread on sandwich. Secure sandwich with 6-inch skewers and slice sandwich into six portions (see photo 4). Serve immediately. Makes 6 servings.

Assembling time: 20 minutes

1 Using a fork, lightly scrape and remove the bread from bottom half of the loaf, as shown. This makes more room for the sandwich filling. Leave a ½-inch-thick shell of crust and bread to give the sandwich support. If desired, also remove some of the bread from the top half of the loaf. Freeze the crumbs for toppings or meat loaf.

2 To remove the stem end from tomato, cut out a cone-shape piece with a sharp knife. To slice the tomato, grasp it with one hand and place it on a cutting board. Use the sharp knife to thinly slice tomato crosswise, as shown.

3 After spreading the bottom half of the loaf with butter, top it with lettuce. Next, layer coleslaw, ham, tomato, drained cucumbers and onions, and salami.

4 Insert 6-inch skewers vertically through the top layer of bread, the filling, and the bottom layer of bread. This helps hold the sandwich together while you slice it. If you can't locate 6-inch skewers, break longer bamboo kabob skewers into 6-inch lengths. Steadying the sandwich with one hand, cut it into portions with a serrated or sharp, thin-bladed knife using a smooth sawing motion, as shown. Remove the skewers before eating.

Cheese and Pastrami Hoagies

There's a little "hot stuff"—pepper cheese and horse-radish mustard—in every bite.

⅓   **cup plain yogurt**
2   **teaspoons horseradish mustard**
4   **French-style rolls (5 to 6 inches long)**
    Butter *or* margarine, softened
1   **small onion**
    Romaine leaves
5   **ounces very thinly sliced pastrami *or* cooked beef**
3   **ounces sliced Monterey Jack cheese with jalapeño peppers**
    Whole sweet cherry peppers *or* whole hot banana peppers (optional)

In a small bowl stir together yogurt and horse-radish mustard, then set aside. Cut rolls in half horizontally. Using a fork, hollow out centers of bottom halves; leave a ½-inch-thick shell (see photo 1, page 8). Spread cut side of bottom halves of rolls with butter or margarine.

Cut onion crosswise into thin slices, then separate into rings. Arrange romaine leaves over bottom halves of rolls. Layer pastrami or beef, cheese, and onion rings over romaine (see photo 3, page 9). Spoon yogurt mixture over onion. Replace top halves of rolls. Secure sandwiches with 6-inch skewers (see photo 4, page 9). Serve with peppers, if desired. Makes 4 servings.

Assembling time: 15 minutes

Deli Salad Sandwiches

12   **slices raisin bread**
1   **pint purchased deli-style chicken *or* ham salad**
1   **8¼-ounce can crushed pineapple, drained**
½   **cup broken pecans**

Toast bread. In a small bowl combine chicken or ham salad, pineapple, and pecans. Spread *each* of six toast slices with about ⅓ *cup* of mixture. Top each with another toast slice. Secure with toothpicks, then cut sandwiches in half (see photo 4, page 9). Serve sandwiches immediately. Makes 6 servings.

Assembling time: 15 minutes

Stuffed Pita Pockets

½   **pint purchased mayonnaise-style potato salad**
2   **teaspoons prepared horseradish**
3   **large pita bread rounds**
1   **medium tomato**
6   **ounces sliced cooked beef *or* fully cooked ham**
6   **slices muenster *or* colby cheese (6 ounces)**
    Lettuce *or* spinach leaves

In a bowl stir together potato salad and horse-radish. Mash mixture slightly with a fork, if desired. Cut pita bread rounds in half crosswise, then separate carefully to form pockets. Cut tomato into thin slices (see photo 2, page 9). To assemble each sandwich half, spoon potato salad mixture into pita pockets, then add beef or ham, cheese, lettuce or spinach, and tomato. Makes 6 servings.

Assembling time: 30 minutes

Easy Reubens

Want to use pita bread instead of rye? Cut two large pita bread rounds in half crosswise, then line them with cheese and lettuce. Add the filling and pickles.

1 **8-ounce can sauerkraut**
8 **ounces thinly sliced cooked corned beef**
⅓ **cup Thousand Island salad dressing**
2 **slices Swiss cheese**
8 **slices rye bread**
   Red-tipped lettuce leaves (optional)
4 **to 8 pickle slices**

Rinse sauerkraut, then drain thoroughly. Snip sauerkraut with scissors, if desired. Tear corned beef into bite-size pieces. In a medium bowl stir together sauerkraut, corned beef, and salad dressing. Cut cheese slices in half.

To assemble sandwiches, place cheese atop *four* of the bread slices. If desired, add a lettuce leaf. Layer corned beef-sauerkraut mixture on top of lettuce, then layer pickle slices on each sandwich (see photo 3, page 9). Top with remaining bread slices. Secure with toothpicks, then cut sandwiches in half (see photo 4, page 9). Makes 4 servings.

Assembling time: 15 minutes

Turkey Club Sandwiches

12 **slices pumpernickel, sourdough, *or* rye bread**
    Prepared mustard
4   **ounces thinly sliced Swiss *or* Monterey Jack cheese**
8   **ounces thinly sliced cooked turkey breast**
½   **cup cranberry-orange relish**
    Lettuce leaves
    Butter *or* margarine (optional)

Toast bread. For top layer, spread *four* of the toast slices with mustard. Layer cheese atop mustard-spread bread. Using *half* of the turkey, layer slices over cheese (see photo 3, page 9).

For bottom layer, spread *four* more toast slices with cranberry-orange relish. Top with lettuce leaves and remaining turkey.

To assemble sandwich, stack cheese-and-turkey layer on top of each relish-turkey layer. Spread remaining toast with butter or margarine, if desired. Place buttered side down on each cheese-and-turkey layer. Secure each sandwich with toothpicks, then cut diagonally into quarters (see photo 4, page 9). Makes 4 servings.

Assembling time: 20 minutes

Assemble A Salad

A main-dish salad is a great choice when you need a refreshing meal on short notice. And when you plan to include some ready-to-use ingredients— such as prepared coleslaw or potato salad, bottled dressing, and canned meat, fruit, or vegetables—it's especially easy to do.

Round out your meal with rolls or crackers, fresh fruit, and a beverage.

Seafood Louis

Seafood Louis

¼ of a 4-ounce container frozen whipped dessert topping
1 7¾-ounce can artichoke hearts
2 eggs
1 large head Bibb lettuce
½ medium head iceberg lettuce
2 large tomatoes
1 cup Thousand Island salad dressing
1 small lemon
6 ounces frozen crab-flavored fish sticks *or* frozen cooked shrimp, thawed

Place topping in a small bowl and thaw. Place can of artichokes in the freezer to chill for 20 minutes (see tip, page 16). To hard-cook eggs, place eggs in a saucepan. Cover with cold water. Bring water to boiling. Reduce heat to just below simmering, then cook, covered, for 15 minutes. Drain and cool eggs (see photo 1).

Meanwhile, rinse Bibb and iceberg lettuce; drain. Shred iceberg lettuce (see photo 2). Cut tomatoes into wedges. Peel and slice eggs. For dressing, stir salad dressing into thawed topping (see photo 3). Cut lemon into wedges.

Cut crab-flavored fish sticks into large pieces. Drain artichokes, then cut into quarters. Assemble salads (see photos 4–7). Spoon dressing over salads. Garnish with eggs. Sprinkle with paprika, if desired. Pass lemon. Serves 4.

Assembling time: 35 minutes

1 To quickly cool hard-cooked eggs, place in a pan of cold water and add ice cubes. Then let eggs stand about 5 minutes. Do this as one of the first steps in preparing the salad, so the eggs will be completely cooled when you're ready to use them.

2 After removing the core and rinsing the lettuce, drain in a colander or on paper towels.
 To shred iceberg lettuce (or cabbage), place the half-head of lettuce on a cutting board. Cut into thin shreds with a long-bladed knife.

3 For the creative, fast-to-fix dressing, in a small bowl stir together Thousand Island salad dressing and thawed topping.

4 Line four chilled, individual luncheon plates with Bibb lettuce leaves.

5 Next, make a pile of shredded iceberg lettuce in the center of each plate.

6 Place crab-flavored fish pieces or shrimp on top of the shredded lettuce.

7 Finally, arrange tomato wedges and artichoke heart quarters on salads.

Chicken-and-Fruit Salad

Replace canned tuna for the canned chicken. Voilà . . . a fruity seafood salad.

1   **8¾-ounce can peach slices**
2   **5-ounce cans chunk-style chicken**
1   **16-ounce can grapefruit sections**
1   **avocado *or* 1 large apple**
   Lemon juice
½   **cup soft-style cream cheese**
½   **teaspoon poppy seed**
4   **cups torn lettuce**

Place cans of peaches, chicken, and grapefruit in the freezer to chill for 20 minutes (see tip below). Meanwhile, halve avocado lengthwise, then twist gently to separate. Remove seed and the peel, then cut avocado into 12 lengthwise slices. Brush avocado with a little lemon juice to prevent darkening. (*Or,* core and cut apple into 12 slices.)

Drain peaches, reserving *3 tablespoons* of syrup. For dressing, stir together reserved syrup, cheese, and poppy seed (see photo 3, page 15). Drain and flake chicken.

Place lettuce on four chilled individual luncheon plates (see photo 4, page 15). Arrange chicken in center of each plate atop lettuce (see photo 5, page 15). Arrange peach and grapefruit sections around edges of the plates (see photo 7, page 15). Arrange avocado or apple slices between chicken and fruit. Drizzle dressing over salads. Serve at once. Makes 4 servings.

Assembling time: 35 minutes

Crunchy Tuna Salad

Oranges, tuna, coleslaw, and nuts . . . an unusual combination but a great flavor.

1   **11-ounce can mandarin orange sections**
1   **9¼-ounce can tuna**
1   **pint purchased coleslaw**
   Lettuce
½   **cup sliced almonds, peanuts, *or* cashews**

Place cans of oranges and tuna in the freezer to chill for 20 minutes (see tip below). Meanwhile, if coleslaw is very wet, drain off excess liquid. Rinse lettuce; drain (see photo 2, page 14). Line four chilled individual salad bowls with lettuce leaves (see photo 4, page 15).

Drain oranges and tuna (see tip, page 21). Break tuna into chunks.

In a bowl gently toss together oranges, coleslaw, and almonds, peanuts, or cashews. Spoon mixture into center of each lettuce-lined bowl (see photo 5, page 15). Make an indentation in center of mixture. Arrange tuna chunks in the indentation. Makes 4 servings.

Assembling time: 30 minutes

A Chilling Fact

Many salads call for chilled canned ingredients. If you're short on time, quick-chill ingredients in the can in the freezer for about 20 minutes. Or, if you can plan ahead, put ingredients in the refrigerator overnight to chill.

Ham and Macaroni Slaw

See photo 2 on page 14 for suggestions on shredding cabbage. However, if you're really short on time, pick up a package of shredded cabbage in the produce section of your supermarket.

1¾   **cups corkscrew macaroni**
¾   **cup mayonnaise *or* salad dressing**
½   **of an 8-ounce carton lemon yogurt**
1   **6-ounce package sliced fully cooked ham**
3   **cups shredded cabbage**
1   **4-ounce package (1 cup) shredded cheddar cheese**
1   **cup seedless red *or* green grapes, halved**

Cook macaroni according to package directions; drain. To chill macaroni quickly, place it in a colander, then set colander in a large bowl of ice water about 3 minutes or till cool.

Meanwhile, for dressing, in a small bowl stir together mayonnaise or salad dressing and lemon yogurt (see photo 3, page 15). Set aside. Cut ham into bite-size strips.

Place ham, cabbage, and cheese in a large salad bowl. Drain macaroni well, then add to cabbage mixture. Pour dressing over cabbage mixture, then toss to coat well. Arrange grapes atop salad. Makes 4 servings.

Assembling time: 25 minutes

Salmon Potato Salad

1   **15½-ounce can salmon**
1   **medium cucumber**
    Lettuce
1   **quart purchased mayonnaise-style potato salad**
1   **2¼-ounce can sliced pitted ripe olives**

Place can of salmon in the freezer to chill for 20 minutes (see tip, page 16). Meanwhile, score cucumber, if desired. To score cucumber, run tines of fork lengthwise along unpeeled cucumber. Slice cucumber; set aside. Rinse lettuce; drain (see photo 2, page 14). Line a 9-inch pie plate with lettuce (see photo 4, page 15). Spoon potato salad atop lettuce in a ring around outside edge of pie plate. Place about *two-thirds* of the cucumber slices around edge. Drain salmon (see tip, page 21). Discard skin and bones. Break salmon into chunks, then place in center. Arrange the remaining cucumber slices around salmon. Drain olives; scatter over salmon. Sprinkle with snipped fresh dillweed, if desired. Makes 4 servings.

Assembling time: 30 minutes

Bread Fix-Ups

Hot breads taste great with cold main-dish salads. Make breads special with a flavored butter.

Consider serving an herb butter that you can keep on hand in the refrigerator: Stir ½ teaspoon dried *thyme,* crushed, and ½ teaspoon ground *sage* into ½ cup softened *butter.* Spread on slices of French bread. To heat the bread, stack slices, wrap in foil, and bake in a 350° oven about 15 minutes.

Off-the-Shelf Recipes

Caught short on time? Create delicious meals at a moment's notice with ingredients right from your cupboards, freezer, and refrigerator shelves.

For example, we prepared this tempting Ham and Shrimp Creole from easy, quick-to-use ingredients such as rice, canned tomatoes and tomato paste, frozen green pepper, frozen shrimp, and cooked or canned meat.

You'll be surprised at how many other recipes are waiting on your shelves. Turn to this chapter for more off-the-shelf main-dish ideas.

Ham and Shrimp Creole

Ham and Shrimp Creole

A 6¾-ounce can of chunk-style ham makes a handy substitute for the cubed meat. Check the tip box at right for preparation information.

1½ **cups quick-cooking rice**
2 **tablespoons butter *or* margarine (optional)**
1 **16-ounce can tomatoes**
1 **6-ounce can tomato paste**
½ **cup water**
⅓ **cup frozen chopped green pepper**
½ **teaspoon dried thyme, crushed**
½ **teaspoon Worcestershire sauce**
¼ **teaspoon bottled hot pepper sauce**
⅛ **teaspoon garlic powder**
1 **6-ounce package frozen cooked shrimp**
6 **ounces fully cooked ham**
   Pickled okra (optional)

Cook rice according to package directions. Stir in butter or margarine, if desired, then keep warm (see photo 1).

Meanwhile, cut up tomatoes (see photo 2). In a large saucepan stir together *undrained* tomatoes, tomato paste, water, green pepper, thyme, Worcestershire sauce, hot pepper sauce, and garlic powder. Bring to boiling. Reduce heat, then simmer, covered, for 20 minutes.

Meanwhile, thaw shrimp (see photo 3). Drain and set shrimp aside. Cut ham into ½-inch cubes (see photo 4). Stir shrimp and ham into tomato mixture. Simmer, uncovered, about 5 minutes more or till shrimp and ham are heated through. Serve over rice. Garnish with pickled okra, if desired. Makes 4 servings.

Assembling time: 10 minutes
Cooking time: 25 minutes

1 Keep cooked rice warm in a covered saucepan. If you like, stir in a couple tablespoons butter. It helps keep the rice grains from sticking together.

2 Save yourself clean-up time by cutting up the large tomato pieces right in the can. Use kitchen shears for quick 'n' easy cutting.

3 To thaw the frozen shrimp, place them in a colander set in your sink. Let warm tap water run over the shrimp about 3 minutes or until thawed. No attention is necessary—just set a timer. You also can thaw frozen vegetables in a minute or two under warm running water.

4 Quickly cube or slice meat by lining up meat strips on a cutting board; cut crosswise all at once, as shown. For ½-inch cubes, first cut a ½-inch-thick piece of meat into ½-inch strips.

To eliminate a bowl, drain canned foods—fish, meat, fruit—right in the can. Using the lid, press against the food; invert to drain. Remove the lid. For meat or fish, break up with a fork, as shown. If you need to remove bones from the fish, drain the fish in the can, then transfer the fish to a bowl.

Potato Shell Turkey Pie

¼ cup butter *or* margarine
½ cup milk
2 cups packaged instant mashed potato
  flakes
  Dash pepper
1 10-ounce package frozen mixed
  vegetables
1 10¾-ounce can condensed cream
  of onion soup
½ cup shredded Swiss cheese (2 ounces)
½ cup milk
¼ teaspoon dried basil, crushed
2 5-ounce cans chunk-style turkey
½ of a 3-ounce can French-fried onions

In a medium saucepan melt butter or margarine. Stir in ½ cup milk. Remove from heat, then stir in potato flakes and pepper. Press potato mixture onto the bottom and up the sides of a greased 10-inch pie plate.

Meanwhile, thaw frozen vegetables (see photo 3, page 20). In a mixing bowl stir together vegetables, soup, cheese, ½ cup milk, and basil.

Drain turkey and break into chunks (see tip, page 21). Layer turkey atop potato crust. Top with soup mixture. Bake in a 350° oven for 20 minutes. Sprinkle top with onion rings. Bake about 5 minutes more or till mixture is heated through. Makes 6 servings.

Assembling time: 20 minutes
Cooking time: 25 minutes

Tuna-Broccoli-Sauced Pastry

For an even faster version, spoon the tuna-broccoli mixture over cheese crackers.

1 9-inch folded frozen *or* refrigerated
  unbaked piecrust
3 cups frozen cut broccoli
1 12½-ounce can tuna
1 10¾-ounce can condensed cream of
  celery soup
¾ cup milk
¾ teaspoon dried basil, crushed

Let piecrust stand at room temperature according to package directions. With a pastry wheel or knife, cut unbaked piecrust into 1-inch pieces. Place pieces, in a single layer, on a greased baking sheet. Bake in a 450° oven 7 to 8 minutes or till golden. Meanwhile, thaw broccoli (see photo 3, page 20). Set aside. Drain tuna and break into chunks (see tip, page 21). Set aside. In a 2-quart saucepan stir together soup and milk; stir in broccoli, tuna, and basil. Cook over medium heat 12 to 15 minutes or till hot, stirring frequently. Spoon mixture over pastry pieces on dinner plates. Serves 6.

Assembling time: 15 minutes
Cooking time: 12 to 15 minutes

Quick Fruit Salads

Need a simple salad suggestion for dinner? Stir up a fruit combo—it's as easy as tossing greens with bottled dressing. Just put several cans of fruit in the refrigerator to chill. At mealtime, drain and mix the fruit, then serve on lettuce-lined salad plates. The results are delicious and a welcome change from a tossed salad.

Seafood and Wild Rice Salad

If you already have crabmeat or shrimp in the freezer, use it in place of the canned seafood.

2   4½-ounce cans shrimp *or* one
      7-ounce can crabmeat
1   6¼- *or* 6¾-ounce package quick-
      cooking long grain and wild rice mix
¼   cup red wine vinegar and oil
      salad dressing
¼   cup chopped green pepper, celery, *or*
      green onion
      Lettuce leaves
      Tomato wedges (optional)
      Avocado slices (optional)

Place canned shrimp or crabmeat in the freezer for 15 minutes to chill. Meanwhile, prepare long grain and wild rice mix according to package directions. To chill rice quickly, place the saucepan in a large bowl or sink of ice water about 5 minutes or till cool, stirring occasionally (see photo 2, page 81).

Transfer rice to a bowl; stir in salad dressing and green pepper, celery, or green onion. Cover and quick chill in the freezer 10 to 15 minutes. Drain seafood (see tip, page 21). Rinse canned shrimp or remove any cartilage from crab.

To assemble salads, line four chilled individual salad plates with lettuce. Spoon on a mound of rice mixture, then top with seafood. Arrange tomato wedges and avocado slices around rice mixture, if desired. Serve at once. Serves 4.

Total preparation time: 30 minutes

Chicken and Corkscrew Macaroni

If you don't have the shapely corkscrew macaroni, plain elbow macaroni works well, too.

2   cups corkscrew *or* elbow macaroni
      (about 6 ounces)
1   7½-ounce can tomatoes
1   15-ounce can tomato sauce
1   4-ounce can sliced mushrooms, drained
¼   cup frozen chopped green pepper
½   teaspoon sugar
½   teaspoon dried Italian seasoning,
      crushed
      Dash pepper
2   5-ounce cans chunk-style chicken
1   cup shredded mozzarella *or*
      Monterey Jack cheese (4 ounces)

Cook macaroni according to package directions. Meanwhile, cut up tomatoes (see photo 2, page 20). In a large saucepan or 10-inch skillet stir together *undrained* tomatoes, tomato sauce, mushrooms, green pepper, sugar, Italian seasoning, and pepper. Bring the mixture to boiling. Reduce heat, then simmer, covered, for 10 minutes, stirring occasionally.

Drain macaroni. Drain canned chicken and break into chunks (see tip, page 21). Stir drained macaroni and chicken into tomato mixture. Heat through. Transfer to a serving dish, then sprinkle with cheese. Makes 4 servings.

Assembling time: 10 minutes
Cooking time: 20 minutes

Easy Corned Beef Stroganoff

3 cups wide *or* medium noodles
 (4 ounces)
1 12-ounce can corned beef, chilled
1 14½-ounce can beef *or* chicken broth
1 4-ounce can sliced mushrooms, drained
1 teaspoon minced dried onion
1 8-ounce carton dairy sour cream
¼ cup all-purpose flour
1 cup frozen peas

Cook noodles according to package directions; drain and keep warm (see photo 1, page 20). Meanwhile, remove corned beef from the can and cut into ½-inch cubes (see photo 4, page 21). Set aside.

In a large saucepan stir together broth, mushrooms, and onion. Cook over medium heat till heated through. Stir together sour cream and flour. Stir sour cream mixture into mixture in saucepan. Bring to boiling, stirring constantly.

Stir corned beef cubes and peas into hot mixture. Cook about 5 minutes more or till peas are tender and meat is heated through. Serve over noodles. Makes 4 servings.

Total preparation time: 30 minutes

Sausage-Vegetable Stew

Choose either the biscuit mix "dumplings" or refrigerated biscuit topper for this delightful main dish.

1 14½-ounce can stewed tomatoes
2 12-ounce packages fully cooked smoked
 sausage links
2 tablespoons cornstarch
1 tablespoon minced dried onion
1 teaspoon instant chicken bouillon
 granules
½ teaspoon dried basil, crushed
1 16-ounce can sliced carrots
½ cup water
1 teaspoon Worcestershire sauce
1 16-ounce can sliced potatoes
1 cup packaged biscuit mix *or*
 1 package (6) refrigerated biscuits
Sesame seed

If necessary, cut up tomatoes (see photo 2, page 20). Cut sausage into ½-inch-thick slices (see photo 4, page 21). In a large saucepan stir together cornstarch, onion, bouillon granules, and basil. Stir in *undrained* tomatoes, *undrained* carrots, water, and Worcestershire sauce. Cook and stir till thickened and bubbly.

Drain potatoes, then stir sausage and potatoes into mixture in saucepan. Cook until hot and bubbly. Meanwhile, if using packaged biscuit mix, prepare drop biscuit batter according to package directions. Pour sausage mixture into a 3-quart casserole. Quickly drop biscuit batter into six mounds atop *hot* mixture. (*Or,* quickly arrange refrigerated biscuits over *hot* mixture.) Sprinkle sesame seed over biscuits. Bake in a 425° oven for 12 to 15 minutes or till biscuits are golden brown. Makes 6 servings.

Assembling time: 15 minutes
Cooking time: 12 to 15 minutes

◀ *Pictured opposite: Sausage-Vegetable Stew*

Hurry-Up Meat Loaves

How can you streamline the cooking time for a meat loaf? Form the meat into a ring or mini loaves— it'll bake faster that way. For even speedier results, use your microwave oven.

If you usually make meat loaf with ground beef, how about giving another type of meat a try and serving a lamb, ham, or pork loaf instead? We've got recipes for all of them on the following pages.

Pizza-Style Meat Loaf

Pizza-Style Meat Loaf

1	**egg**
1	**8-ounce can pizza sauce**
⅓	**cup fine dry bread crumbs**
2	**teaspoons minced dried onion**
1	**teaspoon dried oregano, crushed**
¼	**teaspoon pepper**
1	**pound ground beef**
1	**slice mozzarella cheese (1½ ounces)**

In a medium bowl beat egg slightly. Stir in *½ cup* of pizza sauce, crumbs, onion, oregano, and pepper. Add beef, then mix well. Shape meat into a ring or mini loaves (see photos 1–3). Bake in a 350° oven for 35 minutes. Spoon off fat (see photo 4).

Spoon remaining pizza sauce over meat. Bake about 5 minutes more or till meat is well done (see tip, page 30). Cut cheese into eight triangles. Arrange cheese atop meat. Bake about 1 minute more or till cheese begins to melt. Garnish with cherry tomatoes and parsley, if desired. Makes 4 servings.

Assembling time: 15 minutes
Cooking time: 41 minutes

Microwave Directions

Prepare meat mixture and shape into a ring in a nonmetal pie plate (see photos 1 and 2). Cover and micro-cook on 100% power (HIGH) for 7 to 8 minutes or till done, turning dish (see tip, page 31). Spoon off fat (see photo 4).

Place remaining pizza sauce in a 1-cup glass measure. Micro-cook, loosely covered, on 100% power (HIGH) for 30 to 45 seconds or till heated through, stirring once. Spoon sauce over meat. Arrange cheese on top of sauced meat. Let stand 5 minutes.

1 Mound the meat mixture in a pie plate. Shape it 2 inches high and 5 inches in diameter, as shown. Or, press the meat into a 5-inch-diameter bowl. Then, invert into a pie plate; remove the bowl. Either way gives you the right shape.

2 Form a 2-inch-diameter hole in the center of the meat mound with your hands while maintaining the height of the loaf at 2 inches. The hole in the center shortens baking time because heat can penetrate meat from all sides.

3 Another way to cut baking time is to make mini loaves. With your hands, form four 4x2-inch loaves, then place them in a 10x6x2-inch baking dish.

4 Spoon off any fat that bakes out of the meat loaf. Holding the dish with a pot holder, slightly tilt the baking dish to one side so it's easier to spoon off the drippings. Discard drippings.

Zesty Pork Loaves

1 **egg**
¼ **cup buttermilk**
1½ **cups soft bread crumbs (2 slices)**
1 **cup shredded cheddar cheese (4 ounces)**
½ **teaspoon salt**
¼ **teaspoon ground sage**
⅛ **teaspoon garlic powder**
⅛ **teaspoon dried basil, crushed**
   Dash pepper
1 **pound ground pork**

In a medium bowl beat egg slightly. Stir in buttermilk, crumbs, ¾ *cup* of cheese, salt, sage, garlic powder, basil, and pepper. Add pork, then mix well. Shape meat into four mini loaves (see photo 3, page 29). Bake mini loaves in a 350° oven for 35 minutes. Spoon off fat (see photo 4, page 29). Sprinkle with remaining ¼ cup cheese. Bake about 5 minutes more or till meat is well done and cheese is melted (see tip below). Makes 4 servings.

Assembling time: 20 minutes
Cooking time: 40 minutes

Cook Them Well Done

Because ground meat gets handled more than other meats during processing, cook meat loaves till well done to ensure maximum food safety.

Follow the recipes timings. To check for doneness, cut into the loaves to see that the inside color of the meat is brown. Or, use a meat thermometer to check the cooked meat temperature—it should register 170°F.

Old-Fashioned Meat Loaf

Just like mother used to make . . . only this one uses speedy ingredients—dried onion and parsley.

1 **egg**
½ **cup milk**
½ **cup quick-cooking rolled oats**
2 **teaspoons minced dried onion**
1 **teaspoon dried parsley flakes**
½ **teaspoon salt**
⅛ **teaspoon pepper**
1 **pound ground beef**
¼ **cup catsup**
½ **teaspoon prepared mustard**
½ **teaspoon Worcestershire sauce**

In a medium bowl beat egg slightly. Stir in milk, oats, onion, parsley, salt, and pepper. Add beef, then mix well. Shape meat into a ring (see photos 1 and 2, page 28).

Bake meat ring in a 350° oven for 35 minutes. Spoon off fat (see photo 4, page 29). Combine catsup, mustard, and Worcestershire sauce; spread over meat ring. Bake about 5 minutes more or till meat is well done (see tip at left). Makes 4 servings.

Assembling time: 15 minutes
Cooking time: 40 minutes

Microwave Directions: Prepare meat mixture and shape in a nonmetal pie plate (see photos 1 and 2, page 28). Cover and micro-cook on 100% power (HIGH) for 8 to 9 minutes or till done, turning dish (see tip, page 31). Spoon off fat (see photo 4, page 29).

Combine topping mixture; spread over meat ring. Let stand, covered, for 5 minutes.

Individual Ham Loaves

2 eggs
⅓ cup fine dry bread crumbs
2 tablespoons sliced green onion
2 teaspoons Dijon-style mustard
1 pound ground fully cooked ham
1 10-ounce package frozen peas in cream sauce

In a medium bowl beat eggs slightly. Stir in crumbs, green onion, and mustard. Add ham, then mix well. Shape meat into four mini loaves (see photo 3, page 29). Bake in a 350° oven about 30 minutes. Meanwhile, prepare peas in cream sauce according to package directions. Spoon over loaves. Makes 4 servings.

**Assembling time: 15 minutes
Cooking time: 30 minutes**

Microwave Directions: Prepare meat mixture and shape into mini loaves in a nonmetal baking dish (see photo 3, page 29). Cover and micro-cook on 100% power (HIGH) for 6 to 8 minutes or till done, turning dish (see tip below). Prepare peas and spoon over loaves.

Meat Loaf Microwave Tips

Choose shallow nonmetal baking containers. Waxed paper makes a good cover for the meat during cooking. Give the baking dish a half-turn after 4 minutes of micro-cooking for more even cooking.

Our recipes were tested in countertop microwave ovens that operate on 600 to 700 watts. Times are approximate because ovens vary by manufacturer.

Spinach and Lamb Loaf

Serving yogurt with this dish adds a cool tanginess.

1 10-ounce package frozen chopped spinach, cooked
2 eggs
½ cup milk
½ cup fine dry bread crumbs
¼ cup grated Parmesan cheese
½ teaspoon salt
½ teaspoon dried rosemary, crushed
¼ teaspoon onion powder
⅛ teaspoon pepper
1½ pounds ground lamb
Plain yogurt

Drain spinach. In a medium bowl beat eggs slightly. Stir in spinach, milk, crumbs, cheese, salt, rosemary, onion powder, and pepper. Add lamb, then mix well. In a 10-inch pie plate or 13x9x2-inch baking pan, shape meat into a ring measuring 2 inches high and 8 inches in diameter (see photos 1 and 2, page 28).

Bake in a 350° oven about 40 minutes or till meat is well done (see tip, page 30). Spoon off fat (see photo 4, page 29). Dollop servings with yogurt. Makes 6 servings.

**Assembling time: 25 minutes
Cooking time: 40 minutes**

Microwave Directions: Prepare meat mixture and shape into a ring in a nonmetal pie plate or pizza plate (see photos 1 and 2, page 28). Cover and micro-cook on 100% power (HIGH) for 12 to 14 minutes or till done, turning dish a quarter-turn every 4 minutes (see tip at left). Spoon off fat (see photo 4, page 29). Dollop with yogurt.

Speedy Skillet Suppers

Looking for a fix-it-fast recipe for supper? Search no farther. We've created some tasty one-dish meals for you. Just pick one out and you're on your way to tonight's fuss-free supper.

Making and *serving* our supper dishes is a snap. You toss all the ingredients into a skillet to cook. Then at mealtime, take your skillet to the table for serving. It's all so easy!

Mexicali Skillet

Mexicali Skillet

Sausage time! No need to cook the rice first … it cooks with other ingredients in this skillet meal.

1   **medium onion**
1   **tablespoon cooking oil**
1   **16-ounce can tomatoes**
1   **4-ounce can diced green chili peppers**
1   **15-ounce can pinto beans**
1   **cup water**
⅔   **cup long grain rice**
1   **teaspoon chili powder**
1   **5-ounce package small smoked sausage links *or* 4 fully cooked smoked sausage links, cut into 16 pieces**
1   **cup shredded cheddar cheese (4 ounces)**

Chop onion (see photo 1). In a 10-inch skillet cook onion in hot oil till tender but not brown (see photo 2). Cut up tomatoes. Drain chili peppers. Add *undrained* tomatoes, chili peppers, *undrained* beans, water, and *uncooked* rice to the skillet (see photo 3). Stir in chili powder. Bring to boiling (see photo 4). Reduce heat to medium-low, then simmer, covered, 15 minutes or till rice is nearly tender.

Stir rice mixture thoroughly. Arrange sausage pieces atop mixture (see photo 5). Simmer, covered, 5 minutes more or till sausages are heated through and rice is tender. Sprinkle cheese over mixture in the skillet. Cover and cook about 2 minutes more or till cheese is almost melted. Makes 6 servings.

Assembling time: 15 minutes
Cooking time: 28 minutes

1 To chop onion, use a chef's knife to halve onion from top to root end. Place onion halves, flat side down, on a cutting board. Slice from top to bottom, making the cuts parallel. Then cut across the slices, as shown.

2 Cook and stir onion in hot oil till tender but not brown. The onion pieces will have a translucent appearance.

3 After adding the other ingredients to the skillet, stir in uncooked rice. For these easy skillet dishes, the juice from the vegetables, the broth, or the water that's added to the mixture is the cooking liquid for the rice, pasta, barley, or bulgur.

4 Bring the mixture to boiling over high heat, as shown. (Bubbles will rise to the surface and break.) Reduce heat to medium-low, cover, then continue simmering the mixture.

5 Stir rice mixture before placing the sausage pieces on top. Arrange sausages spoke-fashion, as shown, so that all the pieces fit on top of the mixture.

Salmon Stroganoff Skillet

1 15½-ounce can salmon
1 12-ounce can vegetable juice cocktail
1 10¾-ounce can condensed
    chicken broth
¾ cup water
1 3-ounce can sliced mushrooms
2 tablespoons snipped fresh parsley *or*
    2 teaspoons dried parsley flakes
2 teaspoons minced dried onion
1 teaspoon Worcestershire sauce
½ teaspoon dried basil, crushed
⅛ teaspoon pepper
5 ounces medium noodles
2 tablespoons all-purpose flour
1 8-ounce carton dairy sour cream

Drain salmon (see tip, page 21). Discard skin and bones, then flake fish. Set aside.

In a 10-inch skillet stir together vegetable juice cocktail, broth, water, *undrained* mushrooms, parsley, onion, Worcestershire sauce, basil, and pepper. Stir in *uncooked* noodles (see photo 3, page 34). Bring mixture to boiling (see photo 4, page 35). Reduce heat to medium-low, then simmer, covered, for 12 to 15 minutes or till noodles are tender, stirring once or twice.

Thoroughly stir flour into sour cream, then stir into mixture in the skillet. Cook and stir over medium-high heat till thickened and bubbly, then cook and stir 1 minute more. Stir in salmon, then heat through. Makes 6 servings.

Assembling time: 20 minutes
Cooking time: 22 to 25 minutes

Chicken and Bulgur Skillet

Bulgur is precooked cracked wheat.

1 medium onion
2 tablespoons butter *or* margarine
1 14½-ounce can chicken broth
2 cups broccoli flowerets *or* one 10-ounce
    package frozen chopped broccoli
½ of a 12-ounce package frozen diced
    cooked chicken (1½ cups)
¾ cup bulgur wheat
¼ teaspoon garlic powder

Cut onion into thin wedges. In a 10-inch skillet cook onion in hot butter or margarine over low heat till onion is tender but not brown (see photo 2, page 34). Stir occasionally.

Add broth, broccoli, chicken, bulgur, and garlic powder to the skillet (see photo 3, page 34). Bring mixture to boiling (see photo 4, page 35.) Break up block of frozen broccoli, if used, with a fork. Reduce heat, then simmer, covered, 10 to 12 minutes or till bulgur and broccoli are done. Makes 4 servings.

Assembling time: 10 minutes
Cooking time: 16 to 18 minutes

Freezer-to-Table Skillet Supper

Keep the major ingredients—chicken, vegetables, and rice—on hand in your freezer for this delightful dish.

8   frozen chicken legs *or* thighs*
½   small onion
¼   cup water
3   tablespoons teriyaki sauce *or* soy sauce
1   9-ounce package frozen Italian
      green beans
2   cups frozen crinkle-cut carrots
2   10-ounce packages frozen long grain
      and wild rice
2   tablespoons slivered almonds

Run warm water over frozen chicken and tap lightly on countertop to separate pieces. Chop onion (see photo 1, page 34). In a 12-inch skillet combine onion, water, and teriyaki or soy sauce. Add the frozen chicken. Bring mixture to boiling. Reduce heat, then simmer, covered, about 30 minutes or till chicken is almost tender.

Meanwhile, place beans and carrots in a colander. Run warm water over vegetables till separated (see photo 3, page 20). Add vegetables and frozen rice to chicken in the skillet.

Bring mixture to boiling (see photo 4, page 35). Reduce heat, then simmer, covered, for 10 to 15 minutes more or till chicken and vegetables are tender, stirring once or twice to break up rice. Sprinkle almonds on top. Makes 4 servings.

*__Note:__ If you freeze the chicken pieces separately, they'll be easier to work with. Or, start with fresh chicken pieces. Reduce the cooking time to just 20 minutes before adding the frozen rice and vegetables.

Total preparation time: 60 to 65 minutes

Macaroni-Beef Supper

The chow mein noodles add the crunch to this main-dish-in-a-skillet.

1   pound ground beef
1   16-ounce can cut green beans, drained
1½   cups water
1   7½-ounce can semicondensed
        cream of mushroom soup
2   teaspoons instant beef bouillon
        granules
1   teaspoon minced dried onion
1   teaspoon Worcestershire sauce
¼   teaspoon salt
       Dash garlic powder
       Dash pepper
¾   cup tiny shell macaroni (3 ounces)
1   3-ounce package cream cheese, cubed
1   3-ounce can chow mein noodles

In a 10-inch skillet cook beef till brown. Drain off fat. Stir in beans, water, soup, bouillon granules, onion, Worcestershire sauce, salt, garlic powder, and pepper. Stir in *uncooked* macaroni (see photo 3, page 34).

Bring to boiling (see photo 4, page 35). Reduce heat to medium-low, then simmer, covered, 20 to 25 minutes or until macaroni is tender, stirring once or twice. Stir in cream cheese cubes. Heat and stir until cheese is melted. Sprinkle with chow mein noodles. Makes 4 servings.

Assembling time: 10 minutes
Cooking time: 25 to 30 minutes

Rush Hour Simmer Dinner

Nested vermicelli is an unusually shaped pasta that's been dried in a little bundle resembling a bird's nest. Look for it in the pasta section of your supermarket. To serve, give each person a bundle.

1　**medium onion**
1　**tablespoon cooking oil**
4　**bundles nested vermicelli (about 5 ounces)**
1　**14½-ounce can chicken broth**
1　**teaspoon dried tarragon, crushed**
1　**10-ounce package frozen peas and carrots**
2　**6¾-ounce cans chunk-style chicken, drained and broken up, *or* one 12-ounce package (3 cups) frozen diced cooked chicken**

Slice onion. In a 10-inch skillet cook onion in hot oil till tender but not brown (see photo 2, page 34). Place *uncooked* vermicelli nests in the skillet. Combine chicken broth and tarragon; carefully pour into the skillet. Add peas and carrots; break up. Bring to boiling (see photo 4, page 35). Reduce heat to medium-low, then simmer, covered, for 15 minutes.

Add chicken; simmer, covered, 5 to 10 minutes more or till pasta is tender and chicken is hot. Makes 4 servings.

Assembling time: 10 minutes
Cooking time: 25 to 30 minutes

Tuna-Spaghetti Skillet

Cook spaghetti in an herbed soup mixture till the pasta is al dente—tender but still slightly firm.

1　**medium onion**
1　**tablespoon cooking oil**
1½　**cups water**
1　**10¾-ounce can condensed cream of onion soup**
4　**ounces spaghetti, broken**
½　**teaspoon dried savory, crushed**
1　**10-ounce package frozen cut broccoli**
1　**9¼-ounce can tuna**
1　**2½-ounce jar sliced mushrooms, drained**
2　**tablespoons grated Parmesan cheese**

Chop onion (see photo 1, page 34). In a 10-inch skillet cook onion in hot oil till tender but not brown (see photo 2, page 34). Add water, condensed soup, and *uncooked* spaghetti to the skillet (see photo 3, page 34). Stir in savory. Bring mixture to boiling (see photo 4, page 35). Reduce heat to medium-low, then simmer, covered, for 15 minutes.

Meanwhile, run warm water over broccoli to break up (see photo 3, page 20). Drain and set aside. Drain and flake tuna (see tip, page 21). Gently stir broccoli, tuna, and mushrooms into skillet. Cook, covered, for 5 to 10 minutes more or till spaghetti is done. Sprinkle with Parmesan cheese. Makes 4 servings.

Assembling time: 10 minutes
Cooking time: 25 to 30 minutes

Ham and Spaetzle Skillet

Spaetzle (SHPETS luh) is a dumpling that has an irregular shape. Buy the spaetzle at the supermarket.

1 **medium onion**
1 **tablespoon cooking oil**
2 **cups cubed fully cooked ham**
1 **10¾-ounce can condensed cream of celery soup**
1 **9-ounce package frozen cut green beans**
1 **cup dried spaetzle**
1 **cup water**
¾ **teaspoon caraway seed**

Chop onion (see photo 1, page 34). In a 10-inch skillet cook onion in hot oil till tender but not brown (see photo 2, page 34). Add ham, soup, beans, *uncooked* spaetzle, water, and caraway seed to the skillet (see photo 3, page 34).

Bring to boiling (see photo 4, page 35). Reduce heat to medium-low, then simmer, covered, for 20 minutes. Stir occasionally to prevent sticking. Remove from heat and let stand, covered, 5 minutes. Makes 4 servings.

Assembling time: 10 minutes
Cooking time: 25 minutes
Standing time: 5 minutes

Barley-Sausage Skillet

1 **medium onion**
1 **large carrot**
1 **tablespoon cooking oil**
1 **16-ounce can sauerkraut, rinsed, drained, and snipped**
1 **14½-ounce can beef broth**
12 **ounces fully cooked smoked Polish sausage, cut into 1-inch pieces**
½ **cup quick-cooking barley**
¼ **cup water**
½ **teaspoon dried basil, crushed**
½ **cup shredded cheddar cheese (2 ounces)**

Chop onion (see photo 1, page 34). Shred carrot. In a 10-inch skillet cook onion and carrot in hot oil till tender but not brown (see photo 2, page 34). Add sauerkraut, beef broth, sausage, *uncooked* barley, water, and basil to skillet (see photo 3, page 34). Bring to boiling (see photo 4, page 35). Reduce heat to medium-low, then simmer, covered, for 15 to 20 minutes or till barley is done.

Sprinkle cheese over mixture in the skillet. Cover and let stand 1 to 2 minutes more or till cheese melts. Makes 4 servings.

Assembling time: 15 minutes
Cooking time: 20 to 25 minutes
Standing time: 1 to 2 minutes

Streamlined Soups

You can forget the idea that delicious homemade soups take hours to cook—our recipes don't. They're all hearty main dishes that are ready in 40 minutes or less.

While the soup cooks, arrange some breadsticks, crackers, or crispy French bread in a basket, and you've got a "souper" quick meal ready to enjoy.

Fish Chowder

Fish Chowder

No need to buy and prepare several vegetables for this chowder. Just use a convenient frozen mixture.

1   16-ounce package fresh *or* frozen
    fish fillets
1   16-ounce package loose-pack frozen
    mixed cauliflower, broccoli, and
    carrots
3   cups milk
¼   cup frozen snipped chives
⅛   teaspoon salt
⅛   teaspoon pepper
2   cups light cream
¼   cup all-purpose flour
¼   teaspoon ground nutmeg (optional)
    Plain croutons (optional)

If frozen, thaw fish at room temperature 20 minutes. Meanwhile, cut up large pieces of frozen vegetables, then add to a 4-quart Dutch oven (see photo 1). Add milk, chives, salt, and pepper to the Dutch oven. Cook over medium-high heat, stirring occasionally, just till boiling.

Shake ½ *cup* of the cream and flour together (see photo 2). Stir flour mixture into hot milk-vegetable mixture in the Dutch oven (see photo 3). Add remaining cream. Cook and stir till thickened and bubbly (see photo 4).

With a heavy knife, cut fish into 1-inch pieces (see photo 5). Add fish and nutmeg, if desired, to soup mixture. Cook, stirring occasionally, 5 to 10 minutes more or until fish flakes easily with a fork. Season to taste with salt, if desired. Ladle mixture into soup bowls. Sprinkle with croutons, if desired. Makes 6 servings.

Total preparation time: 35 to 40 minutes

1 To assure even cooking, cut up any large pieces of the frozen vegetables before adding them to the Dutch oven. Then, add vegetables along with milk, chives, salt, and pepper to the Dutch oven.

3 Gradually pour the flour-cream mixture into the Dutch oven with hot milk-vegetable mixture. Be sure to stir constantly while pouring to prevent chowder from becoming lumpy.

4 Cook and stir till thickened and bubbly. Stir constantly to prevent mixture from sticking to the bottom of the pan. When thickened, the mixture will coat a spoon, as shown.

2 Shake flour and part of the cream together in a jar with a screw-top lid, as shown. Shake vigorously to completely combine flour with cream.

　　If you don't have a screw-top jar, use another container with a lid; be sure to keep your finger on the lid while shaking so the cover doesn't come off.

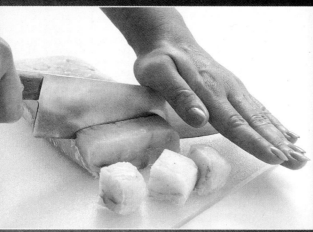

5 Use a heavy knife to cut the fresh or partially thawed fish into 1-inch pieces.

Bratwurst-Potato Chowder

An unusual but delicious way to use a packaged scalloped potato mix.

3 cups water
1 5½-ounce package dry scalloped
  potato mix
1 10-ounce package frozen mixed
  vegetables
12 ounces fully cooked bratwurst
4 cups milk
3 tablespoons all-purpose flour
¼ teaspoon salt

In a 4-quart Dutch oven combine water, potatoes from mix (reserve seasoning packet), and vegetables. Bring mixture to boiling. Reduce heat, then simmer, covered, for 15 minutes, stirring occasionally.

Cut bratwurst into thin slices. Stir bratwurst and *3½ cups* of milk into hot soup mixture in the Dutch oven. Shake remaining ½ cup milk, flour, salt, and seasoning packet from potato mix together (see photo 2, page 43).

Stir flour mixture into soup (see photo 3, page 43). Cook and stir till thickened and bubbly (see photo 4, page 43). Cook and stir 1 minute more. Makes 6 servings.

Total preparation time: 25 minutes

Beer-Cheese Soup

This hearty soup boasts a wonderfully rich, full-bodied cheese flavor.

2½ cups water
1 cup beer
¾ cup small shell macaroni
½ teaspoon instant chicken bouillon
  granules
½ teaspoon minced dried onion
½ teaspoon dried basil, crushed
  Several dashes bottled hot pepper sauce
¼ cup cold water
2 tablespoons all-purpose flour
2 cups shredded American cheese
  (8 ounces)

In a large saucepan combine 2½ cups water, beer, *uncooked* macaroni, bouillon granules, onion, basil, and hot pepper sauce. Bring to boiling. Reduce heat, then simmer, uncovered, for 10 minutes, stirring occasionally.

Shake ¼ cup water and flour together (see photo 2, page 43). Stir flour mixture into hot mixture in the saucepan (see photo 3, page 43). Cook and stir till thickened and bubbly (see photo 4, page 43). Cook and stir 1 minute more. Stir in cheese. Heat and stir till cheese is melted. Makes 4 servings.

Assembling time: 5 minutes
Cooking time: 20 minutes

Savory Beef-Vegetable Soup

Mixed vegetables add the color to this herb-seasoned soup. You even have a choice of herbs!

¾ **pound ground beef**
1 **14½-ounce can beef broth**
1 **8-ounce package frozen mixed vegetables with onion sauce**
¾ **teaspoon dried basil *or* oregano, crushed**
⅛ **teaspoon pepper**
1 **12-ounce can vegetable juice cocktail**
½ **cup cold water**
2 **tablespoons all-purpose flour**

In a large saucepan coarsely crumble ground beef, then cook till brown. Drain off fat. Add broth, vegetables with sauce, basil or oregano, and pepper; mix well. Bring to boiling. Reduce heat, then simmer, covered, for 10 minutes. Stir in the vegetable juice cocktail.

Shake water and flour together (see photo 2, page 43). Stir flour mixture into hot mixture in the saucepan (see photo 3, page 43). Cook and stir till mixture is slightly thickened and is bubbly (see photo 4, page 43). Cook and stir 1 minute more. Makes 4 servings.

Assembling time: 5 minutes
Cooking time: 20 minutes

Herbed Broccoli Soup

Need a recipe for leftover poultry or ham? Here's one with a delicate Swiss cheese flavor.

1 **14½-ounce can chicken broth**
½ **cup finely chopped onion**
¼ **teaspoon dried thyme, crushed**
1 **10-ounce package frozen chopped broccoli**
¾ **cup milk**
¼ **cup all-purpose flour**
1¼ **cups milk**
1½ **cups chopped cooked chicken, turkey, *or* ham**
½ **cup shredded process Swiss cheese (2 ounces)**

In a large saucepan combine broth, onion, and thyme. Add broccoli. Bring to boiling. Reduce heat, then simmer, covered, for 5 minutes.

Shake ¾ cup milk and flour together (see photo 2, page 43). Stir flour mixture into hot broth-vegetable mixture in the saucepan (see photo 3, page 43). Add remaining 1¼ cups milk. Cook and stir till thickened and bubbly (see photo 4, page 43). Cook and stir 1 minute more. Stir in chicken, turkey, or ham and cheese. Heat and stir till meat is heated through and cheese is melted. Makes 4 servings.

Assembling time: 20 minutes
Cooking time: 15 minutes

No-Fuss Oven-Frying

Get out of the kitchen fast! Our speedy solution for easy frying cuts down on KP duty. Put these recipes together in minutes and then leave them alone to cook in the oven. You'll get the flavor of deep-fat frying—without the mess.

We've even simplified cleanup. Put the coating mixture in a plastic bag; add meat, shake to coat, and bake. Just toss out the messy coating bag when you're finished.

Oven-Fried Chicken

Oven-Fried Chicken

You'll need two plastic bags for the coating mixtures.

¼	**cup all-purpose flour**
1	**teaspoon poultry seasoning**
¼	**teaspoon salt**
3½	**cups cornflakes**
2	**tablespoons sesame seed**
1	**egg**
¼	**cup milk**
1	**2½- to 3-pound broiler-fryer chicken, cut up**

In a plastic bag combine flour, poultry seasoning, and salt, then mix well. In another bag coarsely crush cornflakes (see photo 1). Add sesame seed to cereal, then mix well. In a shallow mixing bowl beat egg slightly with a fork, then stir in milk.

Split chicken breast (see photo 2). Cut chicken legs and thighs apart (see photo 3). Rinse chicken, then pat dry with paper towels. Place two or three chicken pieces at a time into bag with flour mixture. Shake well to coat. Dip floured chicken into egg-milk mixture. Coat with crushed cereal mixture (see photo 4).

Place chicken, skin side up and pieces not touching, in a greased 15x10x1-inch baking pan. Repeat with remaining chicken. Bake, uncovered, in a 375° oven for 40 to 50 minutes or till chicken is easily pierced with a fork. *Do not turn.* Makes 6 servings.

Assembling time: 20 minutes
Cooking time: 40 to 50 minutes

1 Place cereal in a large plastic bag. Loosely close bag by folding over end, leaving some room in the bag. Use a rolling pin or crush cereal with your hands. You'll get about half as many crushed crumbs as the original measure of cereal.

2 Store-packaged, cut-up chicken often needs additional cutting. Split the whole chicken breast into two lengthwise pieces through the breastbone. Use a large sharp knife.

3 To split the leg and thigh into two separate pieces, locate the knee joint. Do this by bending the thigh and leg together. Place chicken on a cutting board and cut through the joint.

4 Add the floured and egg-dipped chicken pieces to the bag containing the crumbs mixed with the sesame seed. By adding only a piece or two at a time, each piece gets evenly coated. Roll or gently shake the pieces in the crumb mixture, pressing the crumbs onto the chicken to coat evenly.

Italian Seasoned Chicken Thighs

2 tablespoons butter *or* margarine
15 saltine *or* rich round crackers
1 teaspoon dried Italian seasoning,
   crushed
6 chicken thighs

Preheat oven to 375° for 10 minutes. In a 12x7½x2-inch baking dish heat butter or margarine 5 minutes. Meanwhile, in a plastic bag coarsely crush crackers (see photo 1, page 48). Add Italian seasoning to crumbs, then mix well.

Place chicken in baking dish; turn once to coat surfaces of chicken with butter. Coat chicken with crumb mixture (see photo 4, page 49). Return chicken pieces to baking dish. Bake, uncovered, in the 375° oven for 45 to 50 minutes or till chicken is easily pierced with a fork. *Do not turn.* Makes 3 servings.

Assembling time: 20 minutes
Cooking time: 45 to 50 minutes

Homemade Convenience

Shredding and chopping in double (or more) batches makes good sense. You'll have ingredients ready to use when you need them.

When using the shredder, shred enough cheese for two recipes, instead of one. Tightly wrap the extras; store in the refrigerator.

Or, chop extras when using your chopping board and chef's knife. Onions, green pepper, or nuts are commonly used ingredients that can be chopped in quantity. Chill or freeze for future use.

Corn-Bread-Coated Pork Chops

Mushroom soup serves a dual purpose—it adds flavor and helps the coating mixture cling to the chops.

1⅔ cups corn bread stuffing mix
 ¼ teaspoon ground red pepper
 2 tablespoons butter *or* margarine,
    melted and cooled
 1 7½-ounce can semi-condensed cream
    of mushroom soup
 6 pork chops, cut ¾ inch thick and
    trimmed of separable fat

In a plastic bag combine stuffing mix and red pepper, then mix well. Drizzle butter or margarine over stuffing mixture in bag, then mix well.

Pour soup into a shallow mixing bowl. Dip pork chop into semicondensed soup. Coat with crumb mixture (see photo 4, page 49). Place coated pork chop in an ungreased 15x10x1-inch baking pan.

Repeat with remaining pork chops. Bake, uncovered, in a 375° oven for 45 to 50 minutes or till chops are no longer pink. Makes 6 servings.

Assembling time: 10 minutes
Cooking time: 45 to 50 minutes

Veal Parmigiano

Use canned pizza sauce for a quick meat sauce.

3 tablespoons butter *or* margarine
½ cup fine dry bread crumbs
¼ cup grated Parmesan cheese
⅛ teaspoon salt
1 egg
1 tablespoon milk
¾ pound boneless veal leg round steak,
    cut ¼ inch thick
1 8-ounce can pizza sauce
2 slices mozzarella cheese, halved
    (3 ounces)

Preheat oven to 400° for 10 minutes. In a 13x9x2-inch baking pan heat butter or margarine 5 minutes.

Meanwhile, in a plastic bag combine crumbs, Parmesan cheese, and salt, then mix well. In a shallow mixing bowl beat egg slightly with a fork, then stir in milk. Cut veal into four pieces. Dip one piece of veal into egg-milk mixture. Place into the bag with crumb mixture (see photo 4, page 49). Shake gently to coat all sides.

Place veal in the baking pan atop melted butter. Repeat with remaining veal. Bake, uncovered, in the 400° oven for 10 minutes. Turn veal over. Spoon pizza sauce over veal. Bake about 15 minutes more or till meat is tender. Top with mozzarella cheese. Bake 1 to 2 minutes more or just until cheese melts. Makes 4 servings.

Assembling time: 15 minutes
Cooking time: 27 minutes

Oven-Fried Fish

Select a package of your favorite variety of fish.

1 16-ounce package frozen fish fillets
2 tablespoons butter *or* margarine
½ cup fine dry bread crumbs
½ teaspoon paprika
¼ teaspoon celery salt *or* onion salt
1 egg
    Tartar sauce (optional)

Thaw frozen fish at room temperature for 20 minutes. Meanwhile, preheat oven to 450° for 10 minutes. In an 11x7x1½-inch baking pan heat butter or margarine 5 minutes. In a plastic bag combine crumbs, paprika, and celery or onion salt, then mix well.

Use a sharp knife to cut the block of fish into eight equal portions; pat fish dry. In a shallow mixing bowl beat egg slightly with a fork. Dip one fish portion into beaten egg. Place into the bag with crumb mixture (see photo 4, page 49). Shake gently to evenly coat.

Place fish piece in the baking pan atop melted butter. Repeat with remaining fish. Bake, uncovered, in the 450° oven for 25 to 30 minutes or until fish flakes easily with a fork. Serve fish with tartar sauce, if desired. Makes 4 servings.

Assembling time: 30 minutes
Cooking time: 25 to 30 minutes

Crockery Cooker Meals

For a more relaxed dinnertime, fix most of your evening meal early in the day. How? Use an electric crockery cooker.

Meat and vegetables slowly simmer on their own, developing a savory blend of flavors. The results of no-tend cooking? A deliciously hearty meal that's practically ready to set on the table when your appetite says "Let's eat!"

Barbecue-Style Pork Roast

Barbecue-Style Pork Roast

2 large green peppers
1 large onion
2 stalks celery
1 7½-ounce can tomatoes
1 2½- to 3-pound pork shoulder roast
½ cup bottled barbecue sauce
¼ cup dry red wine
½ teaspoon ground cumin
2 tablespoons cornstarch
2 tablespoons cold water

Thinly cut green peppers into strips and onion into slices. Chop celery. Cut up tomatoes (see photo 2, page 20). In a 3½- or 4-quart electric slow crockery cooker place green peppers, onion, and celery (see photo 1). Add *undrained* tomatoes. Trim excess fat from pork, then cut roast to fit the crockery cooker (see photo 2). Place meat on top of vegetables in the crockery cooker (see photo 3).

In a bowl stir together barbecue sauce, wine, and cumin, then pour over roast. Cover the cooker. Cook on low-heat setting for 9 to 10 hours or till meat and vegetables are tender.

To serve, transfer meat and vegetables to a serving platter and keep warm. Pour liquid into a large glass measure (see photo 4). Skim fat from cooking liquid (see photo 5). Measure *2 cups* cooking liquid; add water, if necessary, to make 2 cups liquid.

For sauce, in a small saucepan stir together cornstarch and water. Stir in 2 cups reserved cooking liquid. Cook and stir till thickened and bubbly, then cook and stir 2 minutes more. Pour sauce over meat and vegetables. Serves 6.

Assembling time: 15 minutes
Cooking time: 9 to 10 hours
Final preparation time: 10 minutes

1 Place the vegetable pieces (sliced, chopped, or cut up) in the bottom of a crockery cooker. They'll keep moist in the meat juices and/or cooking liquid and will cook evenly.

2 If necessary, cut the roast to fit the size of the cooker you are using. A handy cutting guide is the lid of your crockery cooker.

3 Arrange the pieces of meat atop the vegetables in the crockery cooker.

4 For gravy or sauce, remove meat and vegetables from cooker using a meat fork and a slotted spoon or spatula. Transfer to a platter, then cover with foil to keep warm. Pour cooking liquid into a glass measuring cup.

5 Skim fat from the cooking liquid using a spoon. Tip the measure slightly to dip off all the fat; try not to dip off any of the meat drippings.

Turkey Roast with Sweet Potatoes

Reserve half of the turkey for leftovers. One recipe suggestion for leftover turkey is Herbed Broccoli Soup on page 45.

1   3- to 3½-pound frozen boneless
       turkey roast
1   6-ounce can frozen apple juice
       concentrate
3   large sweet potatoes (8 ounces each)
3   inches stick cinnamon
¼   teaspoon whole cloves
¼   cup water
2   tablespoons cornstarch
2   tablespoons cold water

Thaw turkey according to package directions. Thaw apple juice concentrate. Peel potatoes and cut in half lengthwise. In a 3½- or 4-quart electric slow crockery cooker place potatoes (see photo 1, page 55). Add cinnamon and cloves to the cooker. If present, remove gravy packet from roast and save for another use. Place thawed roast on top of potatoes in the crockery cooker (see photo 3, page 55).

Combine apple juice concentrate and ¼ cup water, then pour into the slow cooker. Cover the cooker. Cook on low-heat setting for 9 to 11 hours or until the internal temperature of turkey roast is 185°.

To serve, transfer roast and potatoes to a serving platter and keep warm. Strain juices and pour into a large glass measure (see photo 4, page 55). Skim fat from juices (see photo 5, page 55). Measure *2 cups* juices; add water if necessary. For sauce, in a small saucepan stir together cornstarch and 2 tablespoons cold water. Stir in 2 cups reserved juices. Cook and stir till thickened and bubbly, then cook and stir 2 minutes more. Season to taste with salt and pepper. Pass sauce. Makes 6 to 8 servings.

**Assembling time: thawing time plus
   20 minutes
Cooking time: 9 to 11 hours
Final preparation time: 10 minutes**

Sweet 'n' Sour Chicken Dinner

Puzzled about which chicken pieces are meatiest? They're the breast portions, thighs, and legs.

6   medium carrots, peeled and cut into
       ¼-inch-thick slices
1   large green pepper, seeded and cut into
       1-inch squares
1   medium onion, cut into wedges
3   whole medium chicken breasts, split
       lengthwise, *or* 2½ to 3 pounds meaty
       chicken pieces
¼   teaspoon salt
1   15½-ounce can pineapple chunks,
       drained
1   10-ounce jar sweet-sour sauce
       (about 1 cup)
2   tablespoons cornstarch
2   tablespoons cold water
       Hot cooked rice

In a 3½- or 4-quart electric slow crockery cooker place carrots, green pepper, and onion (see photo 1, page 55). Place chicken atop vegetables in the crockery cooker (see photo 3, page 55). Sprinkle with salt. Pour pineapple and sweet-sour sauce over chicken. Cover the cooker. Cook chicken and vegetables on low-heat setting for 8 to 9 hours or till tender.

To serve, transfer chicken, pineapple, and vegetables to a serving platter and keep warm. Pour juices into a large glass measure (see photo 4, page 55). Skim fat from juices (see photo 5, page 55). Measure *2 cups* juices.

For sauce, in a small saucepan stir together cornstarch and water. Stir in 2 cups reserved juices. Cook and stir till thickened and bubbly, then cook and stir 2 minutes more. Spoon over chicken mixture. Serve with rice. Serves 6.

**Assembling time: 25 minutes
Cooking time: 8 to 9 hours
Final preparation time: 10 minutes**

German-Style Pot Roast

6 **small potatoes (about 1 pound)**
4 **to 6 medium carrots**
1 **medium onion, cut into ¼-inch slices**
1 **3-pound beef chuck roast**
¼ **cup vinegar**
¼ **cup water**
2 **bay leaves**
½ **teaspoon instant beef bouillon granules**
¼ **teaspoon ground cloves**
⅛ **teaspoon garlic powder**
   Cooking oil (optional)
⅓ **cup crushed gingersnaps**

Scrub potatoes. Cut carrots into 2-inch pieces. In a 3½- or 4-quart electric slow crockery cooker place vegetables (see photo 1, page 55). If necessary, cut meat in half to fit the crockery cooker (see photo 2, page 55). Place meat atop vegetables (see photo 3, page 55).

Stir together vinegar, water, bay leaves, bouillon granules, cloves, garlic powder, and ½ teaspoon *salt*. Pour over meat in the cooker. For a moister top, brush surface of meat with a little oil. Cover the cooker. Cook on low-heat setting for 9 to 11 hours or till meat is tender.

To serve, transfer meat and vegetables to a platter and keep warm. Remove bay leaves. Pour juices into a large glass measure (see photo 4, page 55). Skim fat from juices (see photo 5, page 55). Measure *1½ cups* juices; add additional water if necessary. For gravy, pour juices into a small saucepan. Stir gingersnap crumbs into pan juices. Cook and stir till thickened and bubbly, then cook and stir 1 minute more. Slice meat. Pass gravy. Makes 6 servings.

Assembling time: 15 minutes
Cooking time: 9 to 11 hours
Final preparation time: 10 minutes

Beef Sandwiches: Shred leftover beef using two forks; discard fat and bones. For each 1 cup of beef, heat with 3 tablespoons bottled *barbecue sauce*. Serve on *Kaiser rolls or hamburger buns* with *spinach or lettuce leaves.*

Corned Beef and Brussels Sprouts

The sprouts replace cabbage in this old-fashioned dish.

6 **small potatoes**
3 **medium parsnips *or* carrots**
1 **10-ounce package frozen brussels sprouts**
½ **cup water**
2 **bay leaves**
1 **2- to 3-pound corned beef brisket**

Peel potatoes, if desired. Cut parsnips or carrots into 1-inch pieces. In a 3½- or 4-quart electric slow crockery cooker place potatoes and parsnips (see photo 1, page 55). Place frozen brussels sprouts atop vegetables in cooker. Add water and bay leaves. Trim excess fat from brisket. Place meat atop vegetables in the crockery cooker (see photo 3, page 55). Cover the cooker. Cook on low-heat setting for 9 to 10 hours. To serve, transfer meat to a platter, then thinly slice meat across the grain. Discard bay leaves. Serve vegetables with beef. Makes 6 servings.

Assembling time: 20 minutes
Cooking time: 9 to 10 hours

Keep It Covered

Be sure the lid of your slow cooker is on securely during cooking. If it isn't, the food won't cook properly. That's because cooking depends on the heat that builds up in the container itself.

Whenever you lift the cover during cooking, you'll lose heat . . . a quick peek will cool the food 1 or 2 degrees. However, if you leave the cooker uncovered, it can lose as much as 20° of vital cooking heat in only 2 minutes.

Fast Frittatas

Quick-cooking frittatas (*free TAHT ahs*) fit perfectly into jiffy meal plans. These open-faced omelets require few ingredients and little mixing. Unlike the traditional Italian frittatas, our one-step versions eliminate the broiler. Simply add a lid to the skillet and the frittata finishes cooking.

Even serving frittatas is simple. Take your skillet right to the table!

Broccoli Frittata

Broccoli Frittata

Buy shredded cheese to save time and effort.

½ **of a 10-ounce package frozen cut broccoli**
6 **eggs**
⅓ **cup thinly sliced green onion**
¼ **cup light cream or milk**
½ **teaspoon dried savory or marjoram, crushed**
¼ **teaspoon garlic salt**
Dash pepper
1 **tablespoon cooking oil**
½ **cup shredded cheddar or Swiss cheese (2 ounces)**

1 In a medium mixing bowl, lightly beat the eggs with a wire whisk or fork to mix the yolks and whites together, as shown. Eggs should not be frothy.

Thaw broccoli in a colander (see photo 3, page 20). Cut up large broccoli pieces, then set aside. In a mixing bowl lightly beat eggs (see photo 1). Stir in onion, cream or milk, savory or marjoram, garlic salt, and pepper.

In a 10-inch skillet heat oil over medium-low heat till a drop of water sizzles. Add the thawed broccoli to the skillet, then spread evenly. Pour egg mixture into skillet over broccoli (see photo 2). Cook over medium-low heat about 10 minutes. As eggs set, run a spatula around the edge of the skillet, lifting egg mixture to allow uncooked portion to flow underneath (see photo 3). Continue cooking and lifting edge till mixture is almost set (surface will be moist). Remove from heat.

Sprinkle cheese over top of egg mixture. Cover skillet; let stand 3 to 4 minutes or just till cheese is melted and top is set (see photo 4). Cut into wedges. Serve immediately. Makes 4 servings.

Assembling time: 10 minutes
Cooking time: 10 minutes
Standing time: 3 to 4 minutes

2 Spread the thawed broccoli evenly in the skillet with the heated oil. Carefully pour the seasoned egg-cream mixture over broccoli.

3 Use medium-low heat to cook the frittata. Don't let the skillet become too hot or the egg mixture will overcook and become tough. Run a wide spatula around the edge of the skillet as the eggs set, lifting eggs to allow the uncooked portion to flow underneath.

4 Remove the skillet from the heat when the eggs are almost set but still slightly shiny on their top surface. Sprinkle cheese evenly over the eggs. Cover skillet and let frittata stand 3 to 4 minutes. The standing time in a covered pan allows the cheese to melt and the frittata top to finish cooking.

Chicken-Mushroom Frittata

6 eggs
¼ cup milk
1 teaspoon dried parsley flakes
¼ teaspoon salt
¼ teaspoon dried thyme *or* tarragon, crushed
  Dash pepper
1 cup chopped cooked chicken *or* one 6¾-ounce can chunk-style chicken, drained and chopped
3 green onions, sliced
1 2-ounce can chopped mushrooms, drained
1 tablespoon cooking oil

In a mixing bowl lightly beat eggs (see photo 1, page 60). Stir in milk, parsley, salt, thyme or tarragon, and pepper. Stir in chicken, onion, and mushrooms.

In a 10-inch skillet heat oil over medium-low heat till a drop of water sizzles. Pour egg mixture into skillet (see photo 2, page 60). Cook over medium-low heat about 10 minutes. As eggs set, run a spatula around the edge of the skillet, lifting egg mixture to allow uncooked portion to flow underneath (see photo 3, page 61). Continue cooking and lifting edge till mixture is almost set (surface will be moist).

Cover skillet and remove from heat; let stand for 3 to 4 minutes or just till top is set (see photo 4, page 61). Cut into wedges. Serve immediately. Makes 4 servings.

Assembling time: 10 minutes
Cooking time: 10 minutes
Standing time: 3 to 4 minutes

Shrimp Frittata

The shrimp and colorful broccoli flowerets make this egg dish perfect for a special brunch.

1 small onion, chopped
2 tablespoons olive oil *or* cooking oil
1 cup broccoli flowerets
1 4½-ounce can shrimp
6 eggs
¼ cup milk
2 teaspoons soy sauce
  Dash pepper

In a medium saucepan cook onion in *1 tablespoon* of hot oil till onion is tender but not brown. Add broccoli, then reduce heat. Cook, covered, for 5 minutes. Rinse and drain shrimp. Add shrimp to broccoli and onion in saucepan.

In a mixing bowl lightly beat eggs (see photo 1, page 60). Stir in milk, soy sauce, and pepper. Stir in the shrimp mixture.

In a 10-inch skillet heat remaining 1 tablespoon oil over medium-low heat till a drop of water sizzles. Pour egg mixture into skillet (see photo 2, page 60). Cook over medium-low heat about 10 minutes. As eggs set, run a spatula around the edge of the skillet, lifting egg mixture to allow uncooked portion to flow underneath (see photo 3, page 61). Continue cooking and lifting edge till mixture is almost set (surface will be moist).

Cover skillet and remove from heat; let stand 3 to 4 minutes or just till top is set (see photo 4, page 61). Cut into wedges. Serve immediately. Makes 4 servings.

Assembling time: 10 minutes
Cooking time: 18 minutes
Standing time: 3 to 4 minutes

Easy Farmer's Breakfast

3 tablespoons cooking oil
½ of a 24-ounce package (3 cups) frozen hash brown potatoes with onion and peppers
6 eggs
1 cup diced fully cooked ham
¼ cup milk
1 tablespoon frozen chives
¼ teaspoon salt
Few dashes bottled hot pepper sauce
Dash pepper

In a 10-inch skillet heat oil over medium heat. Add frozen potatoes to skillet according to package directions. Cook, covered, for 8 to 10 minutes, stirring once or twice.

Meanwhile, in a mixing bowl lightly beat eggs (see photo 1, page 60). Stir in ham, milk, chives, salt, hot pepper sauce, and pepper. Pour the egg mixture into skillet over potatoes (see photo 2, page 60). Cook over medium-low heat about 10 minutes. As eggs set, run a spatula around the edge of the skillet, lifting egg mixture to allow uncooked portion to flow underneath (see photo 3, page 61). Continue cooking and lifting edge till mixture is almost set (surface will be moist).

Cover skillet and remove from heat; let stand 3 to 4 minutes or just till top is set (see photo 4, page 61). Cut into wedges. Serve immediately. Makes 4 servings.

Assembling time: 10 minutes
Cooking time: 20 minutes
Standing time: 3 to 4 minutes

Pepperoni Frittata

Pepperoni adds flavor in two places—in the frittata itself and in the sauce served over the frittata.

1 3-ounce package cream cheese
1 4-ounce package sliced pepperoni
1 8-ounce can pizza sauce
1 4-ounce can sliced mushrooms, drained
¼ cup milk
6 eggs
¼ teaspoon salt
Dash pepper
2 tablespoons butter *or* margarine

Cut cheese into cubes, then set aside. If pepperoni slices are large, cut them into quarters. In a saucepan combine pizza sauce, mushrooms, and *half* of the pepperoni. Cook over low heat, uncovered, for 10 to 15 minutes.

Meanwhile, in a blender container or food processor bowl combine the cheese cubes and milk. Cover and blend or process till smooth. Add eggs, salt, and pepper. Cover and blend or process 10 seconds. Stir in remaining pepperoni.

In a 10-inch skillet heat butter or margarine over medium-low heat. Pour egg mixture into skillet (see photo 2, page 60). Cook over medium-low heat about 10 minutes. As eggs set, run a spatula around the edge of the skillet, lifting egg mixture to allow uncooked portion to flow underneath (see photo 3, page 61). Continue cooking and lifting edge till almost set (surface will be moist).

Cover skillet and remove from heat; let stand 3 to 4 minutes or just till the top is set (see photo 4, page 61). Cut into wedges. Spoon some pizza sauce mixture over top, then pass remaining sauce. Serve immediately. Makes 4 servings.

Assembling time: 20 minutes
Cooking time: 10 minutes
Standing time: 3 to 4 minutes

Quick-Cooked Frozen Fish

Here's some great news! Don't waste your time waiting for fish to thaw. Instead, poach fish that's still frozen. Then, serve the fish with an easy-to-make sauce or feature it in a main-dish salad.

Save more time—and money, too—by stocking your freezer with a favorite variety of fish. A delicious meal is only minutes and a few footsteps away!

Orange-Poached Fish

Orange-Poached Fish

1 cup long grain rice
1 16-ounce package frozen fish fillets
4 medium carrots
1 stalk celery
1 cup orange juice
¼ teaspoon salt
¼ teaspoon dried basil, crushed
  Dash pepper
1 tablespoon cornstarch
1 tablespoon cold water
  Orange slices
  Cucumber slices

Prepare rice according to package directions. Meanwhile, place frozen block of fish in an ungreased 10-inch skillet. Bias-slice carrots ¼ inch thick and celery ½ inch thick (see photo 1). Add carrots and celery to the fish in the skillet. Stir together orange juice, salt, basil, and pepper, then add to the fish. Bring mixture to boiling. Reduce heat to simmering (see photo 2). Cook, covered, 15 to 20 minutes or till fish tests done (see photo 3).

Spread rice on a warm serving platter. Divide fish into four portions. Remove fish and vegetables from the skillet with a slotted spoon and arrange over rice on the platter. Reserve cooking liquid. Cover platter to keep food warm.

To make sauce, measure cooking liquid (if necessary, add water to measure 1 cup). Strain liquid, if desired, then pour into the skillet. Stir together cornstarch and water, then add to liquid in the skillet. Cook and stir till thickened and bubbly, then cook and stir 2 minutes more. Pour sauce over fish and vegetables. Garnish with orange and cucumber-slice twists (see photo 4). Serve immediately. Makes 4 servings.

Assembling time: 15 minutes
Cooking time: 20 to 25 minutes

1 Bias-slicing gives fresh vegetables extra eye-appeal. And it's so easy. Using a sharp knife, make the first cut on a diagonal. Follow through with the same angle for remaining cuts, slicing vegetables into pieces of even thickness.

3 When the fish is done, it becomes opaque, white, and tender. Test the fish for doneness by inserting fork tines into the fish at a 45-degree angle. Twist the fork gently. The fish is done if it flakes, as shown. If the fish resists flaking and still has a translucent quality, it's not done. If it's dry and mealy, the fish has cooked too long.

2 Bring the orange juice mixture to boiling. Then, reduce heat to simmering. The mixture is simmering when a few bubbles form slowly and burst before they reach the surface. Cover skillet.

4 Decorate the main-dish serving platter with a colorful garnish. Orange and cucumber slices are a quick trim. First, make a cut just to the center of an orange slice. Then, twist the cut ends of the orange in opposite directions. Use the same technique with cucumber (or lemon) slices. For an even more colorful look, twist an orange and a cucumber slice together.

Fish with Cream Sauce

Enhance your favorite fish with this simple, delicate sauce—it's flavored with bay leaves.

  1 **16-ounce package frozen fish fillets**
1½ **cups water**
  2 **tablespoons lemon juice**
  4 **bay leaves**
  1 **teaspoon instant chicken bouillon granules**
⅓ **cup light cream**
  4 **teaspoons cornstarch**
  2 **tablespoons snipped parsley**
      Lemon slices

Place frozen fish in an ungreased 10-inch skillet. Add water, lemon juice, bay leaves, and bouillon granules. Bring mixture to boiling. Reduce heat to simmering (see photo 2, page 67). Cook, covered, 15 to 20 minutes or till fish tests done (see photo 3, page 67). Remove fish from the skillet with a slotted spoon and place on a warm serving platter. Reserve cooking liquid. Cover platter to keep fish warm.

To make sauce, strain 1 cup cooking liquid. Discard remaining liquid and bay leaves. Pour strained liquid into the skillet. Shake cream and cornstarch together (see photo 2, page 43). Stir mixture into the liquid in the skillet. Cook and stir till thickened and bubbly, then cook and stir 2 minutes more. Stir in parsley. Pour sauce over the fish. Garnish with lemon-slice twists (see photo 4, page 67). Makes 4 servings.

Assembling time: 15 minutes
Cooking time: 20 to 25 minutes

Italian-Style Fish

¼ **cup sliced green onion**
  1 **tablespoon cooking oil**
  1 **8-ounce can tomato sauce**
½ **teaspoon sugar**
½ **teaspoon dried thyme, crushed**
⅛ **teaspoon garlic powder**
  1 **pound individually frozen fish fillets**
1½ **cups water**
½ **teaspoon dried basil, crushed**
¼ **cup grated Parmesan cheese**

In a small saucepan cook onion in hot oil till tender but not brown. Stir in tomato sauce, sugar, thyme, and garlic powder. Bring mixture to boiling. Reduce heat, then simmer sauce, uncovered, about 10 minutes.

Meanwhile, place frozen fish in an ungreased 10-inch skillet. Add water and basil. Bring mixture to boiling. Reduce heat to simmering (see photo 2, page 67). Cook, covered, about 4 minutes for ¼-inch-thick fillets (about 8 minutes for ½-inch-thick fillets) or till fish tests done (see photo 3, page 67). Transfer fish to a warm platter. Pour hot sauce over fillets. Sprinkle Parmesan over fillets. Serve immediately. Serves 4.

Assembling time: 10 minutes
Cooking time: 10 minutes

Buying Frozen Fish

Learn to be a smart fish shopper, and you'll never be disappointed with your purchases. Select packages of frozen fish that have their wrappers intact. Also, choose frost-free packages for the best possible product.

Monterey Fish Salad

For extra flavor, use Monterey Jack cheese with jalapeño peppers.

1 **16-ounce package frozen fish fillets**
3 **cups water**
1 **small onion**
1 **stalk celery**
4 **cups torn iceberg lettuce *or*
    romaine**
1 **cup cherry tomatoes, halved**
½ **cup shredded Monterey Jack cheese
    (2 ounces)**
½ **cup bottled Caesar *or* creamy cucumber
    salad dressing**

Place frozen fish in an ungreased 10-inch skillet. Add water to the skillet. Bring water to boiling. Reduce heat to simmering (see photo 2, page 67). Cook, covered, 15 to 20 minutes or till fish tests done (see photo 3, page 67).

Lift fish to a plate with a slotted spoon or spatula. Break fish into 1-inch chunks. Cover and place in the freezer, if desired, to chill while preparing rest of salad.

Cut onion into thin slices and separate into rings. Bias-slice celery ¼ inch thick (see photo 1, page 66). Place lettuce or romaine in a large salad bowl. Add onion rings, celery, and tomatoes. Sprinkle with cheese. Arrange fish chunks on top. Drizzle Caesar or creamy cucumber salad dressing over assembled salad. Lightly toss ingredients together. Makes 4 servings.

Assembling time: 20 minutes
Cooking time: 15 to 20 minutes

Wine-Sauced Fish Steaks

Look no further for a delicious seafood dish that serves just two!

2 **frozen halibut *or* salmon steaks,
    cut ½ to ¾ inch thick
    (about 10 ounces total)**
1½ **cups water**
1 **teaspoon instant chicken bouillon
    granules**
½ **teaspoon dried rosemary, crushed**
1 **10-ounce package frozen rice with peas
    and mushrooms**
2 **tablespoons butter *or* margarine**
1 **tablespoon cornstarch**
¼ **cup dry white wine**
    Parsley sprigs (optional)
    Lemon slices (optional)

Place frozen fish in an ungreased 10-inch skillet. Stir together water, bouillon granules, and rosemary, then add to the fish in skillet. Bring mixture to boiling. Reduce heat to simmering (see photo 2, page 67). Cook, covered, 8 to 10 minutes or till fish tests done (see photo 3, page 67).

Meanwhile, prepare frozen rice according to package directions. Remove fish from the skillet, reserving cooking liquid. Keep fish warm. To make sauce, strain cooking liquid into a glass measure and reserve ¾ cup liquid.

In the same skillet melt butter or margarine. Stir in cornstarch, then stir in ¾ cup reserved cooking liquid. Cook and stir till mixture is thickened and bubbly. Stir in wine, then cook and stir sauce 2 minutes more.

To serve, spread rice mixture on a warm platter. Arrange fish over rice. Spoon sauce over fish. Garnish with parsley and lemon-slice twists, if desired (see photo 4, page 67). Serve immediately. Makes 2 servings.

Assembling time: 15 minutes
Cooking time: 13 to 15 minutes

Versatile Meat Make-Aheads

Saving time by planning ahead is often easier said than done. With these recipes, however, it *is* easy to do. Get much of the work out of the way when you've got some spare time. How?

Make a basic ground meat mixture and freeze it in small portions. Then, when there's little time in your schedule for cooking, build on the base by adding ingredients to make a variety of main dishes.

Hearty Open-Face Sandwiches

Ground Meat Freezer Base

Use half beef and half pork to make a tasty combination of meat flavors.

3 slices bread
3 eggs
1 cup chopped celery
1 cup chopped onion
1 cup shredded carrot
1 teaspoon salt
3 pounds ground beef *or* ground pork

Tear bread slices into quarters, then place in a blender container or a food processor bowl. Cover and blend or process till crumbs are fine and even (see photo 1).

In a large bowl beat eggs. Stir in crumbs, celery, onion, carrot, and salt. Add ground beef or pork and mix well.

In a large skillet cook meat mixture, half at a time, over medium-high heat till meat is brown. Stir to break up large pieces of meat. Drain off fat. Cool quickly (see photo 2).

Spoon about *2 cups* of the meat mixture into *each* of five moisture- and vaporproof containers or freezer bags. Seal, label, and freeze. Makes five 2-cup portions.

Assembling time: 30 minutes
Cooking time: 30 minutes

1 Place bread in a blender container or a food processor bowl. Cover and blend or process till the texture of crumbs is fine and even. Pour crumbs into a measuring cup and measure 2¼ cups.

2 Line a shallow pan with paper towels. Using a slotted spoon, transfer the cooked meat mixture to the paper-lined pan. Spread meat out so that it cools quickly. The paper towels absorb the additional fat that drains off.

Hearty Open-Face Sandwiches

1 **2-cup portion Ground Meat Freezer
   Base (see recipe opposite)**
¼ **cup water**
1 **8¾-ounce can whole kernel corn,
   drained**
¾ **cup bottled barbecue sauce**
4 **wedges corn bread, split, *or* 4 hamburger
   buns, split and toasted**
   Plain yogurt (optional)

Thaw Ground Meat Freezer Base in a 2-quart
saucepan with water (see photo 3). Cover and
cook over medium-low heat about 15 minutes;
break up meat with a fork (see photo 4). Cover
and cook 5 minutes more.

Stir corn and barbecue sauce into meat mixture.
Cook and stir till mixture is heated through.
Spoon meat mixture over corn bread (see pho-
to 5). Or, spoon meat into toasted hamburger
buns. Pass yogurt to spoon on top, if desired.
Makes 4 servings.

Assembling time: 10 minutes
Cooking time: 25 minutes

4 Use a fork to break
apart the frozen
mixture as it begins to
thaw. Breaking it up
speeds the thawing
time. Be sure to use
medium-low heat to
prevent scorching the
mixture during heating.

3 To use a portion
without waiting
hours for it to thaw in
the refrigerator, place
the frozen block of meat
in a saucepan. Then, add
the measured amount
of water.

5 To serve, split
wedges of corn
bread in half and spoon
the hot meat-corn mix-
ture over both halves.
Or, leave the corn bread
wedge or square in one
piece and spoon the
mixture over the top.

Meaty Cream Cheese Stroganoff

If the store doesn't have cream cheese with chives, substitute plain cream cheese. Then, stir in 2 tablespoons of snipped chives.

1   **2-cup portion Ground Meat Freezer Base (see recipe, page 72)**
¼   **cup water**
1   **2½-ounce jar sliced mushrooms, drained**
2   **3-ounce packages cream cheese with chives**
½   **cup milk**
    Hot cooked noodles
    Paprika

Thaw Ground Meat Freezer Base in a 2-quart saucepan with water (see photo 3, page 73). Cover and cook over medium-low heat about 15 minutes; break up meat with a fork (see photo 4, page 73). Cover; cook 5 minutes more.

Stir in mushrooms. Cut cream cheese into cubes, then stir cheese and milk into meat mixture. Cook and stir over low heat till smooth and heated through. Serve over noodles. Sprinkle with paprika. Makes 4 servings.

Assembling time: 5 minutes
Cooking time: 25 to 30 minutes

Skillet Stuffed Peppers

You save valuable time by steaming the green peppers and thawing the meat in the same skillet.

1   **2-cup portion Ground Meat Freezer Base (see recipe, page 72)**
½   **cup water**
2   **medium green peppers**
1   **16-ounce can tomatoes**
½   **cup quick-cooking rice**
1   **teaspoon Worcestershire sauce**
4   **slices American cheese (4 ounces)**

Place Ground Meat Freezer Base in a 10-inch skillet with water (see photo 3, page 73). Cut green peppers in half lengthwise, then discard seeds and membrane. Arrange pepper halves, cut sides down, around edges of the skillet. Cover and cook over medium-low heat about 15 minutes; break up meat with a fork (see photo 4, page 73). Remove green peppers, then drain. Cover and keep warm. Drain off cooking liquid in skillet.

Cut up tomatoes (see photo 2, page 20). Add *undrained* tomatoes, *uncooked* rice, and Worcestershire sauce to meat mixture in the skillet. Bring to boiling. Reduce heat, then simmer, covered, about 5 minutes or till rice is tender.

Put cheese on top of meat mixture. Heat and stir until cheese is melted. To serve, place green pepper halves upright on dinner plates, then spoon in meat mixture. Makes 4 servings.

Assembling time: 10 minutes
Cooking time: 25 minutes

Biscuit-Topped Skillet

Keep ingredients for this dish on hand. Then, when you're in a pinch, fix this meal in about 40 minutes.

1 **2-cup portion Ground Meat Freezer Base (see recipe, page 72)**
¼ **cup water**
1 **10¾-ounce can condensed cream of onion soup**
½ **cup milk**
1 **16-ounce can cut green beans, drained**
1 **8-ounce can sliced water chestnuts, drained**
1 **teaspoon dried basil, crushed**
¼ **teaspoon pepper**
1 **package (6) refrigerated biscuits**

Thaw Ground Meat Freezer Base in a 10-inch oven-going skillet with water (see photo 3, page 73). Cover and cook over medium-low heat about 15 minutes; break up meat with a fork (see photo 4, page 73). Cover and cook the mixture 5 minutes more.

Stir soup and milk into meat mixture. Stir in beans, water chestnuts, basil, and pepper, then heat and stir till bubbly.

Separate each biscuit into two thinner biscuits. Arrange biscuits around edge of *bubbling* meat mixture in the skillet, overlapping to fit. Bake in a 450° oven for 10 to 12 minutes or till biscuits are golden. Makes 4 servings.

Assembling time: 5 minutes
Cooking time: 35 to 37 minutes

Chili-Bean Dish

1 **2-cup portion Ground Meat Freezer Base (see recipe, page 72)**
1 **10-ounce can tomatoes and green chili peppers**
1 **8-ounce can red kidney beans, drained**
1 **8-ounce can tomato sauce**
1 **to 2 teaspoons chili powder**
1 **cup shredded cheddar cheese (4 ounces)**

Thaw Ground Meat Freezer Base in a 2-quart saucepan with ¼ cup *water* (see photo 3, page 73). Cover and cook over medium-low heat about 15 minutes; break up meat with a fork (see photo 4, page 73). Cover and cook 5 minutes more. Stir tomatoes and green chili peppers, kidney beans, tomato sauce, and chili powder into meat mixture in the saucepan. Bring to boiling. Reduce heat, then simmer, uncovered, about 10 minutes or to the desired consistency. Spoon into serving bowls. Sprinkle cheese over each serving. Serve with corn chips, if desired. Makes 4 servings.

Assembling time: 5 minutes
Cooking time: 30 minutes

Thawing the Ground Meat Freezer Base

Thawing times differ slightly depending on whether you freeze the base in a freezer container or bag. It takes about 15 minutes to thaw the block from a freezer container using a little liquid in a pan. Or, shorten the thawing time by freezing the base in a ½- to 1-inch-thick layer in a freezer bag. Thaw base in 5 to 10 minutes.

Oriental Beef

You'll get lots of crunch in this ground meat dish from the water chestnuts and chow mein noodles.

1 **2-cup portion Ground Meat Freezer Base (see recipe, page 72)**
⅔ **cup water**
½ **teaspoon instant beef bouillon granules**
1 **6-ounce package frozen pea pods**
½ **of an 8-ounce can sliced water chestnuts**
2 **tablespoons soy sauce**
2 **tablespoons dry sherry**
1 **tablespoon cornstarch**
½ **teaspoon sugar**
¼ **teaspoon ground ginger *or* five-spice powder**
   Chow mein noodles

Thaw Ground Meat Freezer Base in a 2-quart saucepan with water and bouillon granules (see photo 3, page 73). Cover and cook the mixture over medium-low heat about 15 minutes; break up meat with a fork (see photo 4, page 73). Cover and cook 5 minutes more.

Meanwhile, run warm water over frozen pea pods to separate (see photo 3, page 20). Drain. Add pea pods to meat mixture; cover and cook 2 to 3 minutes more or till heated through. Add water chestnuts.

In a small bowl stir together soy sauce, sherry, cornstarch, sugar, and ginger or five-spice powder. Stir into beef mixture. Cook and stir till thickened and bubbly, then cook and stir 2 minutes more. Serve over chow mein noodles. Makes 3 servings.

Assembling time: 5 minutes
Cooking time: 28 to 30 minutes

Dilled Meat and Potato Chowder

1 **2-cup portion Ground Meat Freezer Base (see recipe, page 72)**
¼ **cup water**
1½ **cups water**
1 **cup sliced potato**
2 **teaspoons instant beef bouillon granules**
½ **teaspoon dried dillweed**
1 **cup milk**
3 **tablespoons all-purpose flour**
⅛ **teaspoon pepper**

Thaw Ground Meat Freezer Base in a 2-quart saucepan with ¼ cup water (see photo 3, page 73). Cover and cook over medium-low heat about 15 minutes; break up meat with a fork (see photo 4, page 73). Cover and cook 5 minutes more.

Drain off cooking liquid. Stir 1½ cups water, potato, bouillon granules, and dillweed into meat mixture. Bring mixture to boiling. Reduce heat, then simmer, covered, for 8 to 10 minutes or till potato is tender.

Meanwhile, combine milk, flour, and pepper in a screw-top jar; shake well (see photo 2, page 43). Stir into beef-potato mixture. Cook and stir till thickened and bubbly, then cook and stir 1 minute more. Makes 4 servings.

Assembling time: 5 minutes
Cooking time: 35 to 40 minutes

Sweet-Sour Beef And Vegetable Salad

While the meat simmers, fix the salad ingredients—spinach or lettuce, mushrooms, and onion. That way, everything's ready to serve at once.

1   **2-cup portion Ground Meat Freezer Base (see recipe, page 72)**
¼   **cup tarragon vinegar**
2   **tablespoons water**
2   **tablespoons lemon juice**
1   **tablespoon cooking oil**
6   **cups torn fresh spinach *or* leaf lettuce (about 8 ounces)**
1   **cup sliced fresh mushrooms**
1   **small onion, thinly sliced and separated into rings**
2   **tablespoons brown sugar**
1   **tablespoon cold water**
1   **teaspoon cornstarch**
1   **11-ounce can mandarin orange sections, drained**

Thaw Ground Meat Freezer Base in a 10-inch skillet with vinegar, 2 tablespoons water, lemon juice, and cooking oil (see photo 3, page 73). Cover and cook over medium-low heat about 15 minutes; break up meat with a fork (see photo 4, page 73). Cover and cook 5 minutes.

Meanwhile, in a large salad bowl combine spinach or leaf lettuce, mushrooms, and onion. Stir together sugar, 1 tablespoon water, and cornstarch; stir into meat mixture. Cook and stir till thickened and bubbly, then cook and stir 2 minutes more.

Spoon meat mixture atop ingredients in salad bowl. Garnish with mandarin oranges. Toss mixture together. Serve immediately. Serves 4.

Assembling time: 5 minutes
Cooking time: 25 minutes

Creamed Peas and Beef

No patty shells on hand? This creamy mixture also tastes fantastic over toast points or biscuits.

4   **frozen patty shells**
1   **2-cup portion Ground Meat Freezer Base (see recipe, page 72)**
¼   **cup water**
1   **10-ounce package frozen peas in cream sauce**
1   **7½-ounce can semi-condensed cream of mushroom soup**
⅓   **cup milk**
1   **2½-ounce jar sliced mushrooms, drained**
1   **tablespoon dry sherry**

Prepare patty shells according to package directions. Meanwhile, thaw Ground Meat Freezer Base in a 2-quart saucepan with water (see photo 3, page 73). Cover and cook over medium-low heat about 15 minutes; break up meat with a fork (see photo 4, page 73). Cover and cook 5 minutes more.

Stir in frozen peas in cream sauce, soup, and milk. Cover and cook 8 to 10 minutes more or till peas are tender, stirring twice.

Stir mushrooms and sherry into mixture. Heat through. Spoon creamed mixture into patty shells. Makes 4 servings.

Assembling time: 5 minutes
Cooking time: 30 to 35 minutes

Double-Duty Entrées

Cook in double batches and you've prepared two meals at once. Serve half now—freeze the other half for dinner number two. The convenience becomes apparent when you discover the minimal preparation and cleanup needed for the second meal. Give our recipes in this section a try. Then use this shortcut trick on some of your own main-dish favorites.

Stew with Potato Topper

Stew with Potato Topper

2 pounds beef stew meat *or* boneless pork,
    cut into 1-inch cubes
2 tablespoons cooking oil
2 cups apple juice *or* apple cider
1 cup water
1½ teaspoons salt
½ teaspoon dried thyme, crushed
¼ teaspoon pepper
1 bay leaf
2 medium onions, cut into wedges
½ cup water
2 tablespoons quick-cooking tapioca
2 teaspoons dried parsley flakes
1 24-ounce package frozen crinkle-cut
    carrots (5½ cups)
1 9-ounce package frozen cut green beans
Packaged instant mashed potatoes
    (enough for 4 servings)
Paprika (optional)

In a 4-quart Dutch oven or large saucepan cook *half* of the meat in hot oil till brown. Remove meat with a slotted spoon; set aside. Repeat with remaining meat. Drain off fat. Return all meat to pan.

Stir in apple juice or apple cider, 1 cup water, salt, thyme, pepper, and bay leaf. Add onions to meat mixture. Bring mixture to boiling. Reduce heat, then simmer, covered, about 1½ hours for beef (or about 45 minutes for pork) or till meat is nearly tender.

Meanwhile, stir together ½ cup water and tapioca; let stand 5 minutes. Stir tapioca mixture and parsley into stew, then add carrots and beans. Return to boiling, stirring occasionally. Reduce heat, then simmer, covered, about 5 minutes more or just till vegetables are tender, stirring occasionally. Discard bay leaf. Transfer *half* of the stew to a pan or bowl (see photo 1). Cool quickly (see photo 2). Transfer to a freezer container; seal, label, and freeze.

Prepare mashed potatoes according to package directions. Ladle remaining hot stew into individual bowls. Spoon potatoes atop stew in large dollops. Sprinkle with paprika, if desired. Makes two portions, 4 servings each.

Assembling time: 30 minutes
Cooking time (beef): 1 hour 35 minutes
    (pork): 50 minutes

To serve the frozen portion: Place freezer container in warm water to loosen stew (see photo 3). Transfer stew to a medium saucepan. Add ¼ cup *water* to saucepan (see photo, page 73). Cook, covered, over medium-low heat 30 to 35 minutes or till thawed, breaking apart with a fork occasionally (see photo 4, page 73). Heat through. Meanwhile, prepare 4 servings packaged instant *mashed potatoes* according to package directions. Serve as above.

Final preparation time: 35 to 40 minutes

1 Using a long-handled measuring cup or a ladle, transfer *half* of the stew to a metal pan or bowl. This portion of stew is cooled and frozen for another meal. Keep remaining stew hot to serve at once.

2 Quickly cool hot stew by placing pan in a larger dish or bowl filled with ice cubes and cold water. Quick cooling is important for food safety. It stops the cooking as well as slows the growth of bacteria in the food. After cooling, immediately transfer mixture to a freezer container.

3 To loosen the frozen mixture from the container, place the covered freezer container in a bowl of warm water. Then, transfer the frozen mixture to a cooking pan.

Mostaccioli with Italian Sauce

Serve some crusty bread or rolls with this main dish.

¾ **pound ground beef**
¾ **pound bulk Italian sausage**
1 **onion, chopped**
1 **clove garlic, minced**
2 **16-ounce cans tomatoes**
1 **8-ounce can tomato sauce**
1 **6-ounce can tomato paste**
2 **teaspoons dried basil, crushed**
1 **3½-ounce package sliced pepperoni**
12 **ounces mostaccioli**
   Grated Parmesan cheese

In a large saucepan cook beef, sausage, onion, and garlic till meat is brown. Drain off fat. Cut up tomatoes (see photo 2, page 20). Stir *undrained* tomatoes, tomato sauce, tomato paste, and basil into meat mixture. Simmer, covered, for 30 minutes. Halve pepperoni slices; stir into meat. Cook 15 minutes more. Skim off fat.

Meanwhile, cook mostaccioli according to package directions till just tender (do not overcook); drain. Place *half* of the mostaccioli (about 2½ cups) in a metal pan or bowl. Pour *half* of the meat mixture (about 4 cups) over mostaccioli in pan (see photo 1, page 81). Stir together. Cool quickly (see photo 2, page 81). Transfer to a freezer container; seal, label, and freeze. Add remaining mostaccioli to remaining meat mixture in saucepan; toss to coat. Pass Parmesan. Makes two portions, 4 servings each.

Total preparation time: 70 minutes

To serve the frozen portion: Place freezer container in warm water to loosen mixture (see photo 3, page 81). Transfer the mixture to a large saucepan. Add ½ cup *water* to saucepan (see photo 3, page 73). Cook, covered, over medium-low heat for 30 to 35 minutes or till thawed, breaking apart with a fork occasionally (see photo 4, page 73). Heat through. Pass grated *Parmesan cheese.*

Final preparation time: 35 to 40 minutes

Saucy Orange Beef

1½ **pounds boneless beef, cut into thin bite-size strips**
2 **tablespoons cooking oil**
1¾ **cups orange juice**
⅓ **cup dry sherry**
¼ **cup soy sauce**
2 **cloves garlic, minced**
½ **teaspoon ground ginger**
3 **tablespoons cornstarch**
1 **8-ounce can sliced water chestnuts, drained**
2 **cups loose-pack frozen mixed green beans, broccoli, onions, and mushrooms**
   Hot cooked rice

In a large skillet brown meat, half at a time, in hot oil. Return all meat to the skillet. Stir in orange juice, sherry, soy sauce, garlic, and ginger. Simmer, covered, for 20 minutes. Combine cornstarch and ⅓ cup *cold water*. Stir into mixture in skillet. Cook and stir till thickened and bubbly, then cook and stir 2 minutes more. Remove from heat. Stir in water chestnuts. Transfer *half* of the mixture to a pan or bowl (see photo 1, page 81). Cool quickly (see photo 2, page 81). Transfer to a freezer container; seal, label, and freeze. Stir the 2 cups vegetables into remaining mixture. Simmer, covered, about 8 minutes or till vegetables are tender. Serve over rice. Makes two portions, 4 servings each.

Total preparation time: 55 minutes

To serve the frozen portion: Place freezer container in warm water to loosen mixture (see photo 3, page 81). Transfer to a saucepan. Add ¼ cup *water* (see photo 3, page 73). Cook, covered, over medium-low heat 20 to 25 minutes or till thawed, breaking apart with a fork (see photo 4, page 73). Stir in 2 cups loose-pack frozen mixed *green beans, broccoli, onions, and mushrooms.* Simmer, covered, about 8 minutes or till vegetables are tender. Serve over hot cooked *rice.*

Final preparation time: 30 to 35 minutes

Shrimp in Cheddar Sauce

Save time by buying shredded cheese.

6 frozen patty shells
1 16-ounce package frozen peas
1 8-ounce package frozen cooked shrimp
½ cup chopped green onion
½ cup butter *or* margarine
⅔ cup all-purpose flour
½ teaspoon paprika
3 cups milk
½ cup dry white wine
2 cups shredded cheddar cheese
    (8 ounces)

Bake patty shells according to package directions. Meanwhile, run warm water over frozen peas. Run warm water over shrimp to thaw (see photo 3, page 20). Drain peas and shrimp well; set aside. In a large saucepan cook onion in butter or margarine till tender. Stir in flour, paprika, and ¼ teaspoon *pepper.* Stir in milk. Cook and stir till thickened and bubbly, then cook and stir 1 minute more. Stir in wine. Add peas and cheese; heat and stir till cheese melts.

Transfer *half* of the mixture to a pan or bowl (see photo 1, page 81). Cool quickly (see photo 2, page 81). Transfer to a freezer container; seal, label, and freeze. Stir shrimp into remaining mixture; heat through. Serve at once in patty shells. Makes two portions, 6 servings each.

Total preparation time: 35 minutes

To serve the frozen portion: Place freezer container in warm water to loosen mixture (see photo 3, page 81). Transfer mixture to a large saucepan. Cook, covered, over medium heat 5 minutes. Reduce heat to medium-low and cook about 20 minutes; stir frequently. Meanwhile, bake 6 frozen *patty shells* according to package directions. Run warm water over one 8-ounce package *frozen cooked shrimp* in a colander; drain well. Add shrimp to mixture in saucepan; cook 10 minutes or till hot. Serve as above.

Final preparation time: 35 minutes

Cranberry-Peach Ham

2 cups frozen crinkle-cut carrots
1½ cups water
1 10-ounce package frozen cranberry-orange relish, thawed
½ cup chili sauce
1½ pounds fully cooked boneless ham, cut into ½-inch cubes
⅓ cup cold water
3 tablespoons cornstarch
1 16-ounce can peach slices, drained
    Hot cooked rice

In a large skillet combine frozen carrots, 1½ cups water, relish, and chili sauce. Bring to boiling. Reduce heat, then simmer, covered, for 10 minutes. Stir in ham.

Combine ⅓ cup water and cornstarch. Stir into mixture in skillet. Cook and stir till thickened and bubbly, then cook and stir 2 minutes more. Transfer *half* of the mixture to a pan or bowl (see photo 1, page 81). Cool quickly (see photo 2, page 81). Transfer to a freezer container; seal, label, and freeze. Cut peach slices in half, if desired. Stir peaches into remaining ham mixture; heat through. Serve over rice. Makes two portions, 4 servings each.

Total preparation time: 35 minutes

To serve the frozen portion: Place freezer container in warm water to loosen mixture (see photo 3, page 81). Transfer mixture to a medium saucepan. Add ¼ cup *water* to saucepan (see photo 3, page 73). Cook, covered, over medium-low heat for 30 to 35 minutes or till thawed, breaking apart with a fork occasionally (see photo 4, page 73). Drain one 16-ounce can *peach slices;* cut slices in half, if desired. Stir peaches into meat mixture; heat through. Serve over hot cooked *rice.*

Final preparation time: 35 to 40 minutes

Broiler Kabobs

The smaller the pieces, the faster the food cooks. That's why kabobs are such a great way to save time. Also, these kabobs are practically a whole meal-on-a-skewer. While the kabobs broil, cook some noodles, toss together a salad, and dinner is ready.

Teriyaki Chicken Kabobs

Teriyaki Chicken Kabobs

1¼ **pounds boneless, skinned chicken breasts**
⅓ **cup teriyaki sauce**
¼ **cup cooking oil**
¼ **cup dry white wine**
1 **tablespoon lemon juice**
¼ **teaspoon onion powder**
2 **stalks celery***
1 **papaya**

Cut chicken into strips (see photo 1). For marinade, in a bowl stir together teriyaki sauce, oil, wine, lemon juice, and onion powder. Add chicken strips, then stir to coat well. Cover and marinate 20 minutes at room temperature or 8 to 24 hours in the refrigerator; stir occasionally.

Preheat the broiler unit. Meanwhile, cut celery into 1-inch pieces. Seed and peel papaya (see photo 2). Cut into 1-inch pieces. Drain chicken strips and reserve marinade. For the kabobs, thread chicken strips alternately with celery and papaya onto eight 8- or 9-inch skewers (see photo 3).

Place kabobs on the *unheated* rack of a broiler pan. Place kabobs 3 to 4 inches from the heat (see photo 4). Broil for 5 minutes. Brush kabobs with reserved marinade (see photo 5). Turn kabobs and brush again with marinade. Broil 5 to 6 minutes more or till chicken is done. Brush again with marinade. Makes 4 servings.

***Note:** If desired, cut 1 large *red or green pepper* into 1-inch squares and substitute for all or part of the celery pieces.

Assembling time: 30 minutes
Marinating time: 20 minutes to 24 hours
Cooking time: 10 to 11 minutes

1 Place boned chicken breasts on a cutting surface. Using a sharp knife, cut chicken into ¾- to 1-inch-wide strips, making the strips as long as possible. The longer the strips, the easier they will be to thread onto the skewers.

2 Select a ripe, yet firm papaya. Prepare papaya by first cutting fruit in half lengthwise. Scoop out the black seeds that fill center cavity. Cut off the thin skin from each half using a small paring knife. Finally, cut the fruit into 1-inch pieces.

3 To thread kabobs, skewer one end of a chicken strip. Next, add a celery, papaya, or pepper piece. Then, thread another portion of chicken strip onto skewer and another fruit or vegetable piece, as shown (top). If strip is long enough, continue with chicken and fruit or vegetable piece. Repeat threading of chicken and fruit and vegetable pieces on the same skewer, as shown (bottom). Repeat for rest of skewers.

4 Place kabobs on the unheated rack of a broiler pan. Place pan under broiler so that the top surface of the kabobs is 3 to 4 inches from the heat source. Use a ruler to measure the distance. If you place kabobs closer than 3 inches, the food will burn instead of cook properly.

5 Baste kabobs with reserved marinade during broiling and just before serving. The marinade adds moistness as well as flavor. Use a long-handled pastry brush for brushing.

Ham and Apricot Kabobs

1 **8¼-ounce can pineapple chunks**
½ **cup apricot preserves**
2 **tablespoons bottled steak sauce**
1 **tablespoon vinegar**
¼ **teaspoon ground cinnamon**
1 **pound fully cooked boneless ham**
2 **green peppers, cut into 1-inch squares**
2 **tablespoons apricot preserves**

Drain pineapple, reserving syrup. For marinade, in a bowl stir together reserved pineapple syrup, ½ cup apricot preserves, steak sauce, vinegar, and cinnamon.

Cut ham into 1-inch cubes. For the kabobs, thread ham alternately with pineapple and green peppers onto eight 9-inch wooden skewers. Place kabobs in a shallow dish. Pour marinade over kabobs. Cover and marinate 20 minutes at room temperature or 8 to 24 hours in the refrigerator; turn kabobs several times.

Preheat the broiler unit. Drain kabobs and reserve marinade. Place kabobs on the *unheated* rack of a broiler pan. Place kabobs 3 to 4 inches from the heat (see photo 4, page 87). Broil for 5 minutes. Brush kabobs with reserved marinade (see photo 5, page 87). Turn kabobs and brush again with marinade. Broil 5 minutes more. Stir together *2 tablespoons* of remaining marinade and 2 tablespoons apricot preserves; brush over kabobs before serving. Makes 4 servings.

Assembling time: 30 minutes
Marinating time: 20 minutes to 24 hours
Cooking time: 10 minutes

Meat and Potato Kabobs

A different twist for meat and potato lovers.

1 **pound boneless beef sirloin steak *or* boneless lamb**
½ **cup cooking oil**
⅓ **cup soy sauce**
¼ **cup lemon juice**
1 **to 2 tablespoons prepared mustard**
1 **to 2 tablespoons Worcestershire sauce**
¼ **teaspoon pepper**
⅛ **teaspoon garlic powder**
2 **small onions**
1 **16-ounce can whole new potatoes, drained**
Paprika (optional)

Cut beef or lamb into 1-inch cubes. For the marinade, in a bowl stir together oil, soy sauce, lemon juice, mustard, Worcestershire sauce, pepper, and garlic powder. Add meat, then stir to coat well. Cover and marinate 20 minutes at room temperature or 8 to 24 hours in the refrigerator; stir occasionally.

Preheat the broiler unit. Meanwhile, cut onions into wedges. Drain meat and reserve marinade. For the kabobs, thread meat alternately with onion wedges and potatoes onto eight 8- or 9-inch skewers.

Place kabobs on the *unheated* rack of a broiler pan. Brush kabobs with reserved marinade. Place kabobs 3 to 4 inches from the heat (see photo 4, page 87). Broil for 5 minutes. Brush kabobs with marinade (see photo 5, page 87). Carefully turn kabobs and brush again with marinade. Broil 6 to 8 minutes more or until meat is desired doneness. Sprinkle potatoes with paprika, if desired. Makes 4 servings.

Assembling time: 15 minutes
Marinating time: 20 minutes to 24 hours
Cooking time: 11 to 13 minutes

Italian Chicken Kabobs

The simple and quick Italian salad dressing marinade adds lots of zippy flavor.

1¼ pounds boneless, skinned chicken breasts
⅔ cup Italian salad dressing
2 tablespoons lemon juice
1 medium green pepper
12 large mushroom caps
Paprika (optional)

Cut chicken into strips (see photo 1, page 86). For marinade, in a bowl stir together Italian salad dressing and lemon juice. Add chicken strips, then stir to coat well. Cover and marinate 20 to 30 minutes at room temperature.

Meanwhile, cut the green pepper into 1-inch squares. Pour *boiling water* over green pepper squares and mushroom caps; let stand 1 to 2 minutes. Drain the pepper squares and mushrooms. Drain chicken and reserve marinade.

Preheat the broiler unit. For the kabobs, thread chicken strips alternately with mushrooms and green pepper onto eight 8- or 9-inch skewers (see photo 3, page 87).

Place kabobs on the *unheated* rack of a broiler pan. Place kabobs 3 to 4 inches from the heat (see photo 4, page 87). Broil for 5 minutes. Brush chicken with reserved marinade (see photo 5, page 87). Turn kabobs and broil 5 to 6 minutes more or till chicken is done. Brush again with marinade. If desired, sprinkle kabobs with paprika before serving. Makes 4 servings.

Assembling time: 15 minutes
Marinating time: 20 to 30 minutes
Cooking time: 10 to 11 minutes

Spicy Pork Kabobs

Skewer fruit and pork for a flavor-winning combination.

1 pound boneless pork
1 8-ounce can pineapple chunks (juice pack)
1 small onion, finely chopped
3 tablespoons soy sauce
1 tablespoon brown sugar
1 tablespoon lemon juice
1 tablespoon cooking oil
1 teaspoon ground coriander
1 teaspoon ground cumin
⅛ teaspoon ground red pepper
1 clove garlic, minced
1 medium zucchini, cut into ¼-inch-thick slices
1 apple, cut into ¼-inch-thick wedges
Hot cooked rice (optional)

Cut pork into 1-inch cubes. Drain pineapple, reserving ¼ cup juice. For marinade, in a bowl stir together reserved pineapple juice, onion, soy sauce, brown sugar, lemon juice, oil, coriander, cumin, red pepper, and garlic. Add meat to marinade, then stir to coat well. Cover and marinate 20 minutes at room temperature or 8 to 24 hours in the refrigerator; stir occasionally.

Preheat the broiler unit. Drain meat and reserve marinade. For the kabobs, thread meat alternately with zucchini, apple, and pineapple onto eight 8- or 9-inch skewers.

Place kabobs on the *unheated* rack of a broiler pan. Brush kabobs with reserved marinade. Place kabobs 3 to 4 inches from the heat (see photo 4, page 87). Broil for 8 minutes. Carefully turn kabobs and brush again with marinade (see photo 5, page 87). Broil 7 to 8 minutes more or till pork is done. Brush with any additional marinade before serving. Serve with rice, if desired. Makes 4 servings.

Assembling time: 25 minutes
Marinating time: 20 minutes to 24 hours
Cooking time: 15 to 16 minutes

Convenient Quiches

Forget piecrust-making forever! With our shortcut quiches, you can skip the pastry-making part.

The luscious quiche you see here starts with a purchased, rolled-out pastry. Or, try a mock crust made with pasta or stuffing mix for other quiches. Sound simple?

The fillings are just as easy . . . and they're deliciously different.

Hearty Italian Quiche

Hearty Italian Quiche

1 9-inch folded frozen *or* refrigerated
    unbaked piecrust
3 eggs
1½ cups milk
¼ cup thinly sliced green onion
½ teaspoon dried oregano, crushed
1 4-ounce package (1 cup) shredded
    mozzarella cheese
1 tablespoon all-purpose flour
3 ounces salami

Let piecrust stand at room temperature according to package directions. Press foil into a 9-inch pie plate (see photo 1). Remove the foil.

Prepare piecrust according to package directions, *except* do not prick. Place foil "shell" atop crust (see photo 2). Bake in a 450° oven for 5 minutes. Carefully remove foil; bake for 5 minutes more. Remove from oven. Reduce oven temperature to 325°.

Meanwhile, in a mixing bowl slightly beat eggs with a rotary beater or wire whisk. Stir in milk, onion, and oregano. Toss together cheese and flour (see photo 3). Chop salami. Stir cheese mixture and salami into egg mixture. Pour into hot piecrust (see photo 4). Bake in a 325° oven for 35 to 40 minutes or till done (see photo 5). Let stand 10 minutes. Makes 6 servings.

Assembling time: 30 minutes
Cooking time: 35 to 40 minutes
Standing time: 10 minutes

1 Press a double thickness of heavy-duty foil into a 9-inch pie plate. Mold foil to the shape of a pie plate. Carefully remove the foil "shell," keeping it in the pie-plate shape.

2 Transfer pastry to the pie plate. Place the foil "shell" atop. Gently press foil against the pastry. The foil helps prevent the pastry from puffing and shrinking during baking.

3 Toss the shredded cheese and the flour together to get the flour evenly distributed. Do this on a piece of waxed paper and there's no bowl to wash!

4 Remove prebaked piecrust from oven and immediately pour filling into the hot crust. Prebaking the crust and adding filling to the hot pastry helps prevent a soggy bottom crust.

5 To test quiche for doneness, insert a knife near center of pie. It should come out clean, as shown. If quiche doesn't test done (some egg mixture remains on knife), bake about 5 minutes longer. Let quiche stand 10 minutes before serving—it will set up more so it'll hold a firmer edge when cut.

Three-Cheese Quiche

Use your blender or food processor to make a smooth cheese filling in lickety-split time.

1 **9-inch folded frozen *or* refrigerated unbaked piecrust**
3 **eggs**
1 **4-ounce package (1 cup) shredded cheddar cheese *or* 1 cup shredded colby cheese (4 ounces)**
½ **cup cream-style cottage cheese**
¼ **cup grated Parmesan cheese**
1 **tablespoon all-purpose flour**
¼ **teaspoon ground red pepper**
1⅓ **cups milk**
½ **of a 3-ounce can French-fried onions**

Let piecrust stand at room temperature according to package directions. Press foil into a 9-inch pie plate (see photo 1, page 92). Remove the foil.

Prepare piecrust according to the package directions, *except* do not prick. Place foil "shell" atop crust (see photo 2, page 92). Bake in a 450° oven for 5 minutes. Carefully remove foil; bake for 5 minutes more. Remove from oven. Reduce oven temperature to 325°.

Meanwhile, in a blender container or food processor bowl combine eggs, cheddar or colby cheese, cottage cheese, Parmesan cheese, flour, and pepper. Cover; blend or process till smooth. Pour into a mixing bowl. Stir in milk. Pour into hot piecrust (see photo 4, page 93). Bake in a 325° oven for 40 to 45 minutes or till done (see photo 5, page 93). Sprinkle onions atop. Let stand 10 minutes. Makes 6 servings.

Assembling time: 30 minutes
Cooking time: 40 to 45 minutes
Standing time: 10 minutes

Quiche in Pasta Crust

The egg that's mixed with the linguine helps the pasta hold its crust shape.

6 **ounces linguine *or* spaghetti**
2 **eggs**
⅓ **cup grated Parmesan cheese**
1 **tablespoon butter *or* margarine, melted**
1 **6-ounce package (1½ cups) shredded Swiss cheese**
2 **eggs**
1 **cup milk**
1 **teaspoon minced dried onion**
⅛ **teaspoon salt**
⅛ **teaspoon garlic powder**
1 **tablespoon all-purpose flour**
3 **tablespoons cooked bacon pieces *or* 4 slices bacon, crisp-cooked, drained, and crumbled**

Cook linguine or spaghetti according to package directions. Drain well. In a mixing bowl beat 2 eggs with a rotary beater or wire whisk. Stir in Parmesan cheese and butter or margarine. Toss drained pasta with egg mixture till well coated.

Press pasta mixture onto bottom and up sides of a well-greased 10-inch quiche dish or pie plate to form a "crust." Sprinkle *1 cup* of the Swiss cheese over crust.

In a mixing bowl slightly beat 2 eggs with a rotary beater or wire whisk. Stir in milk, onion, salt, and garlic powder. Toss together remaining Swiss cheese and flour (see photo 3, page 93). Stir cheese mixture and bacon into egg mixture. Pour into crust. Bake in a 325° oven for 30 to 40 minutes or till done (see photo 5, page 93). Let stand 10 minutes. Makes 6 servings.

Assembling time: 30 minutes
Cooking time: 30 to 40 minutes
Standing time: 10 minutes

Turkey Quiche

If you're tired of making sandwiches from leftover turkey, here's a great way to use up some of the extras!

1 6-ounce package chicken flavor
   stuffing mix
4 eggs
1 5⅓-ounce can (⅔ cup) evaporated milk
⅛ teaspoon dried tarragon, crushed
   Dash pepper
1 6-ounce package (1½ cups) shredded
   Swiss cheese
1 tablespoon all-purpose flour
1 cup chopped cooked turkey *or* chicken

Prepare stuffing mix according to package directions. Press evenly onto bottom and up sides of a 9-inch pie plate to form a crust. Bake in a 400° oven for 10 minutes. Remove from oven. Reduce the oven temperature to 325°.

Meanwhile, in a mixing bowl slightly beat eggs with a rotary beater or wire wisk. Stir in milk, tarragon, and pepper. Toss together cheese and flour (see photo 3, page 93). Stir cheese mixture and turkey or chicken into egg mixture. Pour into hot crust (see photo 4, page 93). Bake in a 325° oven about 40 minutes or till done (see photo 5, page 93). Let stand 10 minutes. Makes 6 servings.

Assembling time: 20 minutes
Cooking time: 40 minutes
Standing time: 10 minutes

Ham and Potato Quiche

½ cup water
¼ cup butter *or* margarine
1½ cups corn bread stuffing mix
½ cup loose-pack frozen hash brown
   potatoes
4 eggs
1 5⅓-ounce can (⅔ cup) evaporated milk
2 teaspoons minced dried onion
1¼ cups shredded cheddar cheese
   (5 ounces)
1 tablespoon all-purpose flour
½ cup diced fully cooked ham

In a saucepan heat water and butter or margarine till butter is melted. Stir in corn bread stuffing mix. Press evenly onto bottom and up sides of a greased 9-inch pie plate to form a crust. Bake in a 400° oven for 15 minutes. Remove from oven. Reduce oven temperature to 325°.

Meanwhile, place hash browns in a sieve or colander. Run warm water over hash browns for 30 seconds or till thawed. Set aside.

In a mixing bowl slightly beat eggs with a rotary beater or wire whisk. Stir in milk and onion. Toss together *1 cup* of the cheese and flour (see photo 3, page 93). Stir potatoes, cheese mixture, and ham into egg mixture. Pour into hot crust (see photo 4, page 93). Bake in a 325° oven about 35 minutes or till done (see photo 5, page 93). Sprinkle with remaining cheese. Let stand 10 minutes. Makes 6 servings.

Assembling time: 25 minutes
Cooking time: 35 minutes
Standing time: 10 minutes

Sensational Stir-Frys

It's no wonder that stir-frying is the most popular Oriental cooking method. It's so quick and easy.

Give stir-frying a try for supper tonight. You don't even need a wok—a large skillet works just as well. Once you've mastered the stir-frying technique, you'll discover countless meat and vegetable combinations you can toss together.

Scallops and Pea Pods

Scallops and Pea Pods

12 ounces fresh *or* frozen scallops
1 6-ounce package frozen pea pods
1 small onion
8 cherry tomatoes
⅓ cup sake *or* dry sherry
¼ cup cold water
2 teaspoons cornstarch
1 teaspoon instant chicken bouillon
    granules
1 teaspoon sugar
1 teaspoon soy sauce
1 teaspoon grated gingerroot *or*
    ¼ teaspoon ground ginger
2 tablespoons cooking oil
    Hot cooked rice

1 Stir-frying is such a quick-cooking process that you need to have all the ingredients ready before you begin. This includes stirring together the cornstarch mixture. Cornstarch settles on bottom of the bowl as it sits. That's why the mixture must be stirred again just before adding to the wok.

Thaw scallops, if frozen, by placing under running water (see photo 3, page 20). Drain well. Cut large scallops in half. Run warm water over frozen pea pods to thaw; drain well. Cut onion into slices and cherry tomatoes in half lengthwise; set aside. In a small bowl stir together sake or sherry, water, cornstarch, bouillon granules, sugar, soy sauce, and gingerroot or ground ginger (see photo 1). Set aside.

Preheat a wok or large skillet over high heat; add *1 tablespoon* of oil (see photo 2). Add onion slices to the wok or skillet. Stir-fry 1 to 2 minutes. Add pea pods, then stir-fry 1 to 2 minutes more or until vegetables are crisp-tender (see photo 3). Transfer vegetables to a bowl.

Add remaining oil to the hot wok or skillet. Add scallops; stir-fry 1 to 2 minutes or till done. Push scallops from center of the wok. Stir cornstarch mixture, then add to the center of the wok or skillet (see photo 4). Cook and stir till thickened and bubbly, then cook and stir 1 minute more. Stir in vegetables. Place tomatoes atop. Cover and cook 1 to 2 minutes more or till heated through. Serve with rice. Makes 4 servings.

Assembling time: 15 minutes
Cooking time: 6 to 10 minutes

2 Place the wok over a burner set on high heat. When the wok is very hot, add the cooking oil in a ring around the upper part of the wok so it coats the sides as it runs to the center of the wok, as shown. If you are using a skillet, add the oil to the center of the skillet, then lift and tilt skillet to coat the bottom with oil.

3 Add onion slices and begin stir-frying. Use a long-handled spoon or cooking spatula. Gently lift and turn the food with a folding motion so it cooks evenly. It's important to keep the food moving at all times, otherwise it will quickly burn. Add pea pods; stir-fry, as shown.

4 Push the cooked food away from the middle of the wok, leaving the center clear of food. Stir cornstarch mixture and add it to center of the wok. Cook and stir till mixture is thickened and bubbly, then cook and stir 1 minute more. This ensures that the thickener is completely cooked.

Easy Chicken Stir-Fry

1 **pound boneless, skinned chicken breasts**
1 **16-ounce package loose-pack frozen mixed French-cut green beans, broccoli, mushrooms, and red pepper**
⅔ **cup cold water**
¼ **cup soy sauce**
1 **tablespoon cornstarch**
½ **teaspoon ground ginger**
2 **tablespoons cooking oil**
   Chow mein noodles

Cut chicken into thin bite-size strips. Run warm water over frozen vegetables till partially thawed (see photo 3, page 20). Drain well. In a small bowl stir together water, soy sauce, cornstarch, and ginger (see photo 1, page 98). Set aside.

Preheat a wok or large skillet over high heat; add *1 tablespoon* of oil (see photo 2, page 98). Add vegetables to the wok or skillet. Stir-fry 2 minutes (see photo 3, page 99). Transfer vegetables to a bowl.

Add remaining oil to the hot wok or skillet. Add *half* of the chicken to the wok or skillet; stir-fry 2 to 3 minutes. Remove chicken. Stir-fry remaining chicken 2 to 3 minutes. Return all the chicken to the wok. Push chicken from the center.

Stir cornstarch mixture, then add to the center of the wok or skillet (see photo 4, page 99). Cook and stir till thickened and bubbly, then cook and stir 1 minute more. Stir in vegetables. Cover and cook 1 minute more. Serve with chow mein noodles. Makes 6 servings.

Assembling time: 15 minutes
Cooking time: 9 to 11 minutes

Cranberry-Orange Turkey Stir-Fry

Serve this saucy mixture over fresh bean sprouts or rice, whichever you prefer. Both are delicious!

12 **ounces boneless turkey breast slices *or* boneless, skinned chicken breasts**
1   **9-ounce package frozen Italian green beans**
1   **8-ounce can jellied cranberry sauce**
¼   **cup orange juice**
3   **tablespoons soy sauce**
2   **tablespoons cold water**
4   **teaspoons cornstarch**
2   **tablespoons cooking oil**
4   **cups fresh bean sprouts *or* 2 cups hot cooked rice**

Cut turkey or chicken into thin bite-size strips. Run warm water over frozen green beans to thaw (see photo 3, page 20). Drain well. In a small bowl combine cranberry sauce, orange juice, soy sauce, water, and cornstarch. Mix ingredients together with a fork till combined (see photo 1, page 98). Set aside.

Preheat a wok or large skillet over high heat; add *1 tablespoon* of oil (see photo 2, page 98). Add green beans to the wok or skillet. Stir-fry 2 to 3 minutes (see photo 3, page 99). Transfer beans to bowl. Add remaining oil to the hot wok or skillet. Add turkey or chicken; stir-fry 3 to 4 minutes. Push poultry from center of the wok.

Stir cranberry mixture, then add to the center of the wok or skillet (see photo 4, page 99). Cook and stir till thickened and bubbly, then cook and stir 1 minute more. Stir in green beans. Cover and cook 1 minute more.

Place bean sprouts in colander; run hot tap water over sprouts till warmed. Serve cranberry-poultry mixture over bean sprouts or rice. Makes 4 servings.

Assembling time: 10 minutes
Cooking time: 8 to 10 minutes

Chicken Liver Stir-Fry

Add a crisp salad and a colorful vegetable to round out this main dish.

5 ounces wide noodles (4 cups)
½ cup chicken broth
¼ cup dry white wine
1 tablespoon cornstarch
½ teaspoon dried thyme, crushed
¼ teaspoon salt
⅛ teaspoon garlic powder
1 large green pepper
1 small onion
¾ pound chicken livers
2 tablespoons cooking oil

Cook noodles according to the package directions. Drain and keep warm. Meanwhile, in a bowl stir together broth, wine, cornstarch, thyme, salt, and garlic powder (see photo 1, page 98). Set aside. Cut green pepper into 1-inch squares. Cut onion into thin wedges. Cut large chicken livers in half.

Preheat a wok or large skillet over high heat; add *1 tablespoon* of oil (see photo 2, page 98). Add green pepper and onion to the wok or skillet, then stir-fry 1 to 2 minutes (see photo 3, page 99). Transfer vegetables to a bowl. Add remaining oil to the hot wok or skillet. Add chicken livers to the wok or skillet. Stir-fry 3 to 4 minutes or till just pink.

Push livers from center of the wok. Stir cornstarch mixture, then add to the center of the wok or skillet (see photo 4, page 99). Turn heat to medium-low. Cook and stir till thickened and bubbly. Stir in vegetables. Cover and cook 2 minutes more over low heat. Serve at once over noodles. Makes 4 servings.

Assembling time: 10 minutes
Cooking time: 12 minutes

No-Chop Shrimp Stir-Fry

These frozen shrimp and vegetables need no cutting— they're ready to use when you're ready to cook.

⅔ cup long grain rice
12 ounces fresh *or* frozen shelled shrimp
1 16-ounce package loose-pack frozen mixed green beans, broccoli, onions, and mushrooms
½ cup cold water
¼ cup soy sauce
¼ cup dry sherry
1 tablespoon cornstarch
¼ teaspoon crushed red pepper
⅛ teaspoon garlic powder
2 tablespoons cooking oil
¼ cup peanuts

Prepare rice according to the package directions. Meanwhile, thaw shrimp, if frozen, by placing under running water (see photo 3, page 20). Drain well. Run warm water over frozen vegetables till partially thawed; drain well.

In a small bowl stir together cold water, soy sauce, sherry, cornstarch, red pepper, and garlic powder (see photo 1, page 98). Set aside.

Preheat a wok or large skillet over high heat; add *1 tablespoon* of oil (see photo 2, page 98). Add partially thawed vegetables to the wok or skillet. Stir-fry 2 to 3 minutes or till vegetables are just tender (see photo 3, page 99). Transfer vegetables to a bowl.

Add remaining oil to the hot wok or skillet. Add shrimp; stir-fry 3 to 5 minutes or till shrimp turn pink. Push shrimp from the center of the wok. Stir cornstarch mixture, then add to the center of the wok or skillet (see photo 4, page 99). Cook and stir till thickened and bubbly, then cook and stir 1 minute more. Stir in vegetables and peanuts. Cover and cook about 1 minute more or till heated through. Serve the shrimp-vegetable mixture with rice. Makes 4 servings.

Assembling time: 10 minutes
Cooking time: 20 minutes

Ham and Pecan Stir-Fry

1   8-ounce can pineapple chunks
    (juice pack)
¾   pound fully cooked ham
1   medium green pepper
2   tablespoons soy sauce
2   tablespoons dry sherry
2   teaspoons cornstarch
¼   to ½ teaspoon crushed red pepper
2   tablespoons cooking oil
½   cup pecan halves
    Hot cooked rice

Drain pineapple, reserving juice. Cut ham into bite-size strips. Cut green pepper into 1-inch pieces. In a small bowl stir together reserved pineapple juice, soy sauce, sherry, cornstarch, and red pepper (see photo 1, page 98). Set the mixture aside.

Preheat a wok or large skillet over high heat; add *1 tablespoon* of oil (see photo 2, page 98). Add pecans to the wok or skillet. Stir-fry 30 seconds or till toasted; remove from wok. Add green pepper, then stir-fry 1 minute (see photo 3, page 99). Transfer green pepper to a bowl.

Add remaining oil to the hot wok or skillet. Add ham; stir-fry 2 minutes. Push ham from the center of the wok. Stir cornstarch mixture, then add to the center of the wok or skillet (see photo 4, page 99). Cook and stir till thickened and bubbly, then cook and stir 1 minute more. Stir in green pepper, pineapple, and pecans. Cover and cook 1 to 2 minutes more or till heated through. Serve with rice. Makes 4 servings.

Assembling time: 15 minutes
Cooking time: 7 to 8 minutes

Teriyaki-Sauced Beef And Zucchini

Make cutting easier. Partially freeze the beef before slicing into thin strips.

¾   pound beef top round steak
2   medium zucchini
¼   cup bottled teriyaki sauce
2   tablespoons orange juice
2   teaspoons cornstarch
1   teaspoon minced dried onion
2   tablespoons cooking oil
    Hot cooked rice

Cut beef into bite-size strips. Thinly slice zucchini. In a small bowl stir together teriyaki sauce, orange juice, cornstarch, and onion (see photo 1, page 98). Set aside.

Preheat a wok or large skillet over high heat; add *1 tablespoon* of oil (see photo 2, page 98). Add zucchini to the wok or skillet. Stir-fry 1 minute (see photo 3, page 99). Transfer zucchini to a bowl.

Add remaining oil to the hot wok or skillet. Add beef; stir-fry 2 to 3 minutes. Push beef from the center. Stir cornstarch mixture, then add to the center of the wok or skillet (see photo 4, page 99). Cook and stir till thickened and bubbly, then cook and stir 1 minute more. Stir in zucchini. Cover and cook 1 to 2 minutes more or till heated through. Serve over rice. Serves 4.

Assembling time: 20 minutes
Cooking time: 6 to 8 minutes

Mustard-Sauced Liver

1 **pound beef liver**
8 **ounces broccoli**
¼ **cup cold water**
2 **tablespoons soy sauce**
1 **tablespoon dry mustard**
1½ **teaspoons cornstarch**
1 **teaspoon sugar**
½ **teaspoon instant beef bouillon granules**
⅛ **teaspoon onion powder**
3 **tablespoons cooking oil**
1 **medium tomato, cut into wedges**
  Chow mein noodles

Cut liver into bite-size pieces. Cut broccoli into ½-inch pieces. In a small bowl stir together water, soy sauce, dry mustard, cornstarch, sugar, bouillon granules, and onion powder (see photo 1, page 98). Set aside.

Preheat a wok or large skillet over high heat; add *1 tablespoon* of oil (see photo 2, page 98). Add broccoli to the wok or skillet. Stir-fry 3 minutes (see photo 3, page 99). Transfer broccoli to a bowl.

Add another tablespoon of oil to the hot wok or skillet. Add *half* of the liver; stir-fry 2 to 3 minutes or till liver is done. Remove liver. Add remaining oil. Stir-fry remaining liver 2 to 3 minutes. Return all liver to wok. Push liver from center of the wok.

Stir cornstarch mixture, then add to the center of the wok or skillet (see photo 4, page 99). Cook and stir till thickened and bubbly, then cook and stir 30 seconds more. Stir broccoli and tomato into liver mixture. Cover and cook 1 to 2 minutes more or till heated through. Serve over chow mein noodles. Makes 6 servings.

Assembling time: 15 minutes
Cooking time: 10 to 13 minutes

Sausage-Onion Stir-Fry

Polish sausage, lots of onion, and bulgur or noodles make this a robust main dish.

1 **pound fully cooked smoked Polish sausage**
3 **medium onions**
1 **10-ounce package frozen cauliflower**
½ **cup cold water**
⅓ **cup dry sherry**
2 **tablespoons soy sauce**
1 **tablespoon cornstarch**
⅛ **teaspoon garlic powder**
⅛ **teaspoon pepper**
1 **tablespoon cooking oil**
  Hot cooked bulgur *or* noodles

Cut sausage into ¼-inch slices. Cut onions into thin wedges. Run warm water over frozen cauliflower to thaw (see photo 3, page 20). Drain well. Cut up any large pieces. In a small bowl stir together water, sherry, soy sauce, cornstarch, garlic powder, and pepper (see photo 1, page 98). Set aside.

Preheat a wok or large skillet over high heat; add oil (see photo 2, page 98). Add onions to the wok or skillet. Stir-fry 3 minutes. Add cauliflower and stir-fry 3 to 4 minutes more or till onions and cauliflower are tender (see photo 3, page 99). Transfer vegetables to a bowl.

Add sausage to wok and stir-fry 2 minutes. Push sausage from the center of the wok. Stir cornstarch mixture, then add to the center of the wok or skillet (see photo 4, page 99). Cook and stir till thickened and bubbly, then cook and stir 1 minute more. Stir in vegetables. Cover and cook 1 minute more or till heated through. Serve over bulgur or noodles. Makes 4 servings.

Assembling time: 15 minutes
Cooking time: 11 to 12 minutes

Skip-a-Step Pasta

Luscious lasagna and marvelous manicotti dishes have finally been simplified . . . just for you, the busy cook.

Skip the time-consuming steps of cooking the pasta and sauce separately. Instead, bake all the ingredients together in a single dish. The results are fantastic!

Zucchini Lasagna

Zucchini Lasagna

1 **cup ricotta cheese**
1 **egg**
1 **cup shredded mozzarella cheese**
   (4 ounces)
¼ **cup grated Parmesan cheese**
1 **14½-ounce can stewed tomatoes, cut up**
1 **tablespoon cornstarch**
1 **tablespoon minced dried onion**
1 **teaspoon dried oregano, crushed**
6 **lasagna noodles**
2 **cups shredded zucchini**
   (about 1½ medium zucchini)
½ **cup shredded mozzarella cheese**
   (2 ounces)
⅔ **cup boiling water**

In a mixing bowl stir together ricotta cheese and egg. Stir in 1 cup mozzarella cheese and Parmesan cheese. Stir together *undrained* tomatoes, cornstarch, onion, and oregano.

Place *2* of the *uncooked* lasagna noodles in a 10x6x2-inch baking dish (see photo 1). Layer with *half* of the tomato mixture. Arrange *2* more *uncooked* noodles in the dish. Spread ricotta mixture atop (see photo 2). Top with remaining noodles, zucchini, and remaining tomato mixture. Sprinkle with ½ cup mozzarella cheese.

Slowly pour boiling water into the dish around the entire inside edge (see photo 3). Cover tightly with foil. Bake in a 350° oven for 60 to 65 minutes or till done (see photo 4). Let stand, covered, for 10 minutes. Makes 6 servings.

Assembling time: 20 minutes
Cooking time: 60 to 65 minutes
Standing time: 10 minutes

1 Lay two lasagna noodles, side by side, in the bottom of the baking dish. You may need to break a piece off each noodle so it fits neatly in the baking dish.

2 Spread all of the ricotta mixture over the second layer of uncooked lasagna noodles. Use a rubber spatula to help spread the mixture.

3 Make a little "ditch" around the noodle mixture along the edge of the baking dish. Then, carefully pour boiling water into this "ditch." The water is essential for cooking the pasta properly.

4 To test noodles for doneness, either prick them or drag a fork across them to see if they are tender. Re-cover dish, then let mixture stand so it holds a better cut edge.

Spaghetti Sauce Lasagna

Buy the mozzarella cheese already shredded and you'll save even more time.

1   15½-ounce jar spaghetti sauce with meat
¾   teaspoon dried basil, crushed
⅛   teaspoon garlic powder
2   eggs
1½ cups cream-style cottage cheese, drained
¼   cup grated Parmesan cheese
1   tablespoon dried parsley flakes
¼   teaspoon pepper
⅛   teaspoon salt
6   lasagna noodles
1½ cups shredded mozzarella cheese (6 ounces)
½   cup boiling water

Combine spaghetti sauce, basil, and garlic powder; set aside. In a mixing bowl slightly beat eggs. Stir in cottage cheese, Parmesan cheese, parsley flakes, pepper, and salt.

Place *2* of the *uncooked* lasagna noodles in a 10x6x2-inch baking dish (see photo 1, page 106). Layer with *one-third* of the spaghetti sauce mixture, *half* of the cottage cheese mixture, and *½ cup* mozzarella cheese. Repeat the layers of *uncooked* noodles, spaghetti sauce mixture, cottage cheese mixture, and mozzarella cheese. Top with remaining noodles, spaghetti sauce mixture, and mozzarella cheese.

Slowly pour boiling water into dish around the entire inside edge (see photo 3, page 107). Cover tightly with foil. Bake in a 350° oven for 60 to 65 minutes or till done (see photo 4, page 107). Let stand, covered, for 10 minutes. Serves 6.

Assembling time: 20 minutes
Cooking time: 60 to 65 minutes
Standing time: 10 minutes

Chicken Lasagna

Gone are the days when lasagna noodles come in just one flavor—choose either whole wheat or spinach noodles for variety.

1   cup cream-style cottage cheese
1   3-ounce package cream cheese, softened and cut up
1   10¾-ounce can condensed cream of mushroom soup
1   cup loose-pack frozen cut broccoli
⅓   cup sliced celery
¼   cup milk
1   teaspoon minced dried onion
¼   teaspoon dried oregano, crushed
⅛   teaspoon ground sage
6   lasagna noodles
1   cup chopped cooked chicken *or* turkey
½   cup shredded cheddar cheese (2 ounces)
⅔   cup boiling water

In a mixing bowl stir together cottage cheese and cream cheese; set aside. In a mixing bowl combine soup, broccoli, celery, milk, dried onion, oregano, and sage; set aside.

Place *2* of the *uncooked* lasagna noodles in a 10x6x2-inch baking dish (see photo 1, page 106). Layer with *half* of the cottage cheese mixture and *one-third* of the soup mixture. Repeat layers of noodles, cottage cheese mixture, and soup mixture. Top with remaining noodles, chicken or turkey, and remaining soup mixture. Sprinkle with cheddar cheese.

Slowly pour boiling water into dish around the entire inside edge (see photo 3, page 107). Cover tightly with foil. Bake in a 350° oven for 60 to 65 minutes or till done (see photo 4, page 107). Let stand, covered, for 10 minutes. Serves 6.

Assembling time: 25 minutes
Cooking time: 60 to 65 minutes
Standing time: 10 minutes

Mexican Manicotti

Tastes like a chili dog, but the pasta takes the place of the hot dog bun.

10 frankfurters (1 pound)
10 manicotti shells
½ cup boiling water
2 15-ounce cans chili with beans
1 cup taco sauce
1 cup shredded Monterey Jack *or* cheddar cheese (4 ounces)

Place *1* frankfurter in *each uncooked* manicotti shell. Place the filled shells, so they are not touching, in a 12x7½x2-inch baking dish. Slowly pour boiling water into the dish around the entire inside edge (see photo 3, page 107).

Stir together chili and taco sauce. Spoon atop the filled shells. Sprinkle with cheese. Cover tightly with foil. Bake in a 350° oven for 60 to 65 minutes or till shells are done (see photo 4, page 107). Let stand, covered, for 10 minutes. Makes 6 servings.

Assembling time: 15 minutes
Cooking time: 60 to 65 minutes
Standing time: 10 minutes

Pizza Manicotti

¾ pound ground beef
1 small onion, chopped
1 15-ounce can pizza sauce
⅛ teaspoon garlic powder
Dash pepper
1 cup shredded Monterey Jack *or* mozzarella cheese (4 ounces)
8 manicotti shells
1⅓ cups boiling water
2 tablespoons sliced pitted ripe olives

In a 10-inch skillet cook beef and onion till meat is brown and onion is tender. Drain off fat. Stir ¼ *cup* pizza sauce, garlic powder, and pepper into meat mixture. Bring to boiling. Reduce heat, then simmer 5 minutes. Stir in cheese till melted. Let cool 5 minutes. Spoon mixture into *uncooked* manicotti shells.

Place shells in a 10x6x2-inch baking dish so they are not touching each other. Slowly pour boiling water into the dish around the entire inside edge (see photo 3, page 107). Reserve ½ *cup* pizza sauce. Pour the remaining sauce over shells, spreading to cover shells. Cover tightly with foil. Bake in a 350° oven for 60 to 65 minutes or till shells are done (see photo 4, page 107). Let stand, covered, for 10 minutes.

Meanwhile, in a small saucepan heat reserved pizza sauce. Pour over manicotti. Sprinkle with olives. Makes 4 servings.

Assembling time: 25 minutes
Cooking time: 60 to 65 minutes
Standing time: 10 minutes

Fix-and-Forget Oven Meals

Does taking some time off while preparing a meal sound appealing? Well, here's the secret. Just bake several dishes together in the oven. Once they're cooking, take it easy while the food tends itself. Just follow our timetable on page 114 for the menu preparation steps. Another secret... save on cleanup by using an oven cooking bag to roast the chicken.

Menu

- Lemon-Herbed Chicken*

- Baked Squash with Peas*

- Tossed salad

- Rolls and butter

- Deep-Dish Apple Pie*

*see pages 112-115

Lemon-Herbed Chicken
Baked Squash with Peas
Deep-Dish Apple Pie

Lemon-Herbed Chicken

2	**tablespoons butter *or* margarine**
3	**tablespoons lemon juice**
1½	**teaspoons dried rosemary *or* tarragon, crushed**
1	**3-pound broiler-fryer chicken**
	Garlic salt
1	**tablespoon all-purpose flour**
	Oven cooking bag

Melt butter or margarine. Stir lemon juice and rosemary or tarragon into melted butter or margarine. If desired, tie legs of chicken together and twist wings under back. Sprinkle chicken with garlic salt.

Sprinkle flour in the oven cooking bag according to package directions. Place chicken in prepared bag. Pour in lemon-butter mixture (see photo 1). Close bag. Turn bag to coat chicken with lemon-butter mixture (see photo 2).

Place cooking bag with chicken, breast side up, in a 10x6x2-inch baking dish. Cut slits in top of bag according to package directions (see photo 3). Place chicken in a 375° oven (see photo 4). Bake for 65 to 70 minutes or till done. Remove chicken from bag and transfer to a serving platter (see photo 5). Discard juices and cooking bag. Makes 6 servings.

Assembling time: 15 minutes
Cooking time: 65 to 70 minutes

1 Sprinkle flour in the oven cooking bag to prevent bag from bursting. Place chicken in the prepared bag, then pour the herbed butter mixture over the chicken.

2 Close bag using the closure included in the oven cooking bag package. Turn bag with both hands, coating the entire chicken with the herbed butter mixture so the whole chicken is flavored.

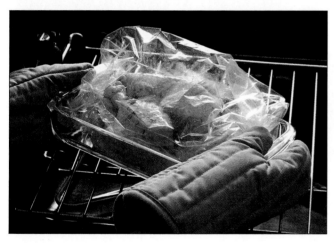

3 Place cooking bag with chicken, breast up, in the 10x6x2-inch baking dish. Make small slits in top of the cooking bag following manufacturer's directions. This lets steam escape.

4 The chicken is the longest cooking item for the menu, so add it to the oven first. Place it to one side of the oven, leaving space for the other dishes you want to include in your oven meal.

5 At serving time, carefully remove chicken from the cooking bag with a fork and wide spatula; transfer the bird to a serving platter. Use the spatula under the chicken and a fork to help you lift it to the platter.

Timetable

1¾ hrs. before
- Remove piecrust from the refrigerator or freezer. Stir together filling for pie. Cut squash for Baked Squash with Peas, as shown. Put in baking pan.
- Get the Lemon-Herbed Chicken ready for the oven, then set it aside. Prepare salad greens; cover them with dampened paper towels to keep the greens crisp. Place in refrigerator to chill.

70 min. before
- Set chicken into a preheated 375° oven, placing dish to one side of the oven. Complete the apple pie, up to the baking step; flute crust to the sides of the dish as shown.

60 min. before
- Arrange the apple pie and the baking pan with the squash halves in the oven on the same rack as the chicken.

At Serving Time
- Cook the frozen peas with onions for the squash filling. Remove chicken, squash, and dessert from the oven. Transfer chicken to a serving platter, as shown. Fill squash halves with cooked peas and onions; place on the serving platter. Toss dressing and salad together. Place rolls in basket.

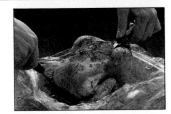

Baked Squash with Peas

A simple but spectacular vegetable dish to include in other oven meals. It has only two main ingredients. (Pictured on page 111.)

3 small acorn squash
(about 14 ounces each)
Salt
Pepper
1 10-ounce package frozen peas with
pearl onions

Split squash in half using a heavy knife. Remove and discard seeds from squash halves. Sprinkle inside of squash halves with salt and pepper.

Place the squash halves, cut side down, in a 13x9x2-inch baking pan. Bake in a 375° oven for 55 to 60 minutes or till squash tests done.

About 10 minutes before serving, cook peas with onions according to package directions. To serve, spoon hot peas with onions into squash halves. Makes 6 servings.

Assembling time: 10 minutes
Cooking time: 55 to 60 minutes

Deep-Dish Apple Pie

Let the pie cool to eating temperature while you enjoy the main course. (Pictured on page 111.)

1 9-inch folded frozen *or* refrigerated
unbaked piecrust
⅔ cup sugar
2 tablespoons quick-cooking tapioca
1½ teaspoons ground cinnamon
¼ teaspoon finely shredded lemon peel
or dried lemon peel
2 20-ounce cans sliced apples
2 tablespoons butter *or* margarine
Sugar
**Light cream *or* vanilla ice cream
(optional)**

Let piecrust stand at room temperature according to package directions. Cut slits in the center of the piecrust.

Meanwhile, in a small mixing bowl stir together ⅔ cup sugar, tapioca, cinnamon, and lemon peel. Drain *1 can* of apples. In a large mixing bowl combine drained and *undrained* apple slices and sugar mixture; toss together well to coat apples. Let stand 10 to 15 minutes.

Turn apple mixture into a 1½-quart casserole. Dot with butter or margarine. Place piecrust over dish. Trim crust to 1 inch beyond the edge of the casserole dish. Fold under the extra inch of pastry. Flute crust to sides of dish, but not over edge. Sprinkle sugar lightly over crust.

Bake in a 375° oven for 55 to 60 minutes or till crust is golden. Serve warm with cream or ice cream, if desired. Makes 6 servings.

Assembling time: 30 minutes
Cooking time: 55 to 60 minutes

Peach Crisp

½ **cup quick-cooking rolled oats**
⅓ **cup packed brown sugar**
¼ **cup all-purpose flour**
½ **teaspoon ground cinnamon**
¼ **cup butter *or* margarine**
1 **16-ounce package frozen unsweetened peach slices**
2 **tablespoons sugar**
⅓ **cup chopped walnuts**
  Vanilla ice cream (optional)

For topping, in a mixing bowl stir together oats, brown sugar, flour, and cinnamon. Cut in butter or margarine until mixture resembles coarse crumbs; set aside. Place frozen peaches in an 8x8x2-inch baking dish *or* an 8x1½-inch round baking dish. Sprinkle sugar and oat mixture over peaches. Sprinkle nuts on top. Bake in a 350° oven for 1 hour. Serve warm with ice cream, if desired. Makes 4 servings.

Assembling time: 15 minutes
Cooking time: 1 hour

Swiss Steak Dinner Timetable

About 2 hours before serving, prepare Oven Swiss Steak. Then, 1¼ hours before serving, place steak and 4 medium baking potatoes in the oven. Prepare Peach Crisp and add to oven.

  Just before serving, cook green beans and top lettuce wedges with salad dressing. Remove dessert from oven; let cool during dinner. Remove meat and potatoes from the oven; transfer to a serving platter. Prepare sauce for meat.

Oven Swiss Steak

The round steak bakes in a wonderfully seasoned, stewed tomato mixture.

1 **pound beef round steak, cut ¾ inch thick**
2 **tablespoons all-purpose flour**
¼ **teaspoon celery salt**
  Dash pepper
2 **tablespoons cooking oil**
1 **small onion**
1 **8-ounce can stewed tomatoes**
2 **teaspoons Worcestershire sauce**
½ **teaspoon Kitchen Bouquet (optional)**
⅛ **teaspoon garlic powder**
1 **tablespoon cold water**
2 **teaspoons cornstarch**

Cut beef into 4 serving-size pieces. Stir together flour, celery salt, and pepper. Use a meat mallet to pound the seasoned flour mixture into beef. In a 10-inch skillet cook meat on both sides in hot oil till brown.

Meanwhile, slice onion and separate into rings. In a bowl stir together onion; *undrained* tomatoes; Worcestershire sauce; Kitchen Bouquet, if desired; and garlic powder. Transfer meat to a 10x6x2-inch baking dish. Pour tomato mixture over meat. Cover dish with foil. Place in a 350° oven (see photo 4, page 113). Bake for 1¼ hours or till tender.

Transfer meat to a serving platter (see photo 5, page 113). Skim fat from tomato mixture. For sauce, in a small saucepan stir together water and cornstarch; stir in tomato mixture. Cook and stir till thickened and bubbly, then cook and stir 2 minutes more. Spoon sauce over meat. Makes 4 servings.

Assembling time: 20 minutes
Cooking time: 1¼ hours
Final preparation time: 5 minutes

▶ *Pictured opposite: Oven Swiss Steak, Peach Crisp*

Shortcut Buymanship

Become a savvy grocery shopper, and you can make every minute count. Supermarkets offer remarkable one-stop shopping. They're stocked with a wide variety of foods . . . and they provide timesaving in-store bakeries, delicatessens, and many nonfood departments.

If you're interested in making the most of your shopping time, read on. These suggestions are meant to help you polish your grocery shopping skills.

Become a Planner
There's no way around it. A key to saving time at the grocery store is to plan ahead.

Prepare an organized shopping list—it'll save you considerable time by eliminating a lot of unnecessary backtracking at the supermarket. Group items on your list by food categories, such as dairy products, produce, canned fruits and vegetables, cereals, meat, frozen foods, nonfood items, staples, and baked goods.

Think about the layout of the store where you regularly shop. Then, organize your list following the store plan. If the produce counter is the first place on your route through the store, start your list with fresh fruits and vegetables.

Make out your grocery list at the same time you plan your menus. By doing this, you will have the ingredients on hand for specific recipes you plan to prepare.

A shopping list also saves you time because it lists *all* the items you need. There's no chance of forgetting a needed ingredient and having to make a time-consuming return trip to the store.

Jot It Down
Keep your shopping list handy to write down commonly used items as they run low. You'll never be disappointed because you ran out of an essential ingredient you "always have on hand" and "can't cook without" if you keep an up-to-date list of grocery needs.

Attach the list with a magnet to your refrigerator door . . . that way, you'll always know where your shopping list can be found.

Also remind family members to add to the list when they come across an item that needs replenishing on the next shopping trip.

Buy Convenience
Invest in convenience foods—those items that are partially or completely prepared.

When available, buy ingredients in the form you'll need for a recipe. For example, purchase sliced or shredded cheese, frozen chopped onion or green pepper, cut-up meat, chopped nuts, bread crumbs, and cracker crumbs for recipe use. These convenient ingredients may cost you a little more—but remember, time is money!

There are other convenience foods that will save you time and work. Frozen juice concentrates; canned soups; canned meat, fish, and poultry; and quick-cooking rice are all timesaving ingredients you might include in your meals.

Shopping Time
To shop quickly, bypass supermarket aisles that offer items you don't need.

A final timesaving reminder . . . shop when others don't! By avoiding the busy times of the week, such as weekends and after work, you save minutes at the checkout counter and avoid aisles that are crowded.

The Know-How Of Freezing

Save both time and money simultaneously. How? Keep a stash of food in the freezer and eliminate time-consuming trips to the supermarket. And take advantage of a bargain . . . buy food when it's on sale, then store it in your freezer.

The secret to good freezer use is knowing the right way to wrap and store foods. After all, you've got an investment at stake, so keep food at its best.

Wrap It, Seal It, And Label It

To protect your frozen food, use moisture- and vaporproof wraps. These protective wraps include the familiar shiny foil, laminated freezer wrap (heavy freezer paper), and polyethylene freezer bags.

Once the food is wrapped, seal packages with freezer tape. Buy the tape along with other freezing materials at your supermarket.

If you've ever gone to the freezer and pulled out an unlabeled mystery package, you know the reason for labeling. The date is important, too. Foods have a storage time limit; for best flavor and quality, they should be used before the time has expired.

Keep an Ongoing List

Another freezing must . . . keep an inventory of items in the freezer. A large sheet of paper and pencil attached to the freezer door will make the job easier. If you categorize the foods

(beef, pork, bread, cake, etc.), you'll be able to quickly spot what you're looking for on the list. Remember to update the list with new purchases and cross off items as you use them.

Protect Your Meat Investment

Because meat is a big-ticket item, you need to take special care when freezing it. For short-time freezer storage (up to 2 weeks), it's okay to freeze fresh meat as it comes packaged in the plastic supermarket wrap. Do a package check to make sure the wrap hasn't been punctured. If it's been damaged, rewrap or overwrap with the freezing materials mentioned previously. Check out the easy wrapping directions at right. If you're not sure how soon you'll use the prepackaged meat, it's best to overwrap the store-wrapped package.

Maintain the freezer temperature at 0° F. or lower. A thermometer placed in the freezer is a good way to check the temperature.

Wrap for Freezing The Easy Way

To wrap meat (and any other solid foods), use the simple technique shown above.

1. Place food in the center of moisture- and vaporproof wrap that's about 1½ times the circumference of the food. Bring the opposite sides of wrap together.

2. Fold the edges down in a series of locked folds. Press the wrap tightly against the meat, pressing out air.

3. Crease the ends into points.

4. Fold the ends up snugly to the center of the package; seal with freezer tape. Label.

How Long Can You Store Meat?

Freeze fresh, uncooked meat and poultry at 0° F. Store:

- beef steaks and roasts 6 to 12 months;
- pork chops 3 to 4 months;
- pork and veal roasts 4 to 8 months;
- lamb chops and roasts 6 to 9 months;
- ground meats 3 to 4 months;
- chicken pieces 9 months;
- turkey pieces 6 months;
- giblets 3 to 4 months;
- whole chickens and turkeys 12 months.

Nutrition Analysis Chart

Use these analyses to compare nutritional values of different recipes. This information was calculated using Agriculture Handbook Number 456, published by the United States Department of Agriculture, as the primary source.

In compiling the nutrition analyses, we made the following assumptions:
- For all of the main-dish meat recipes, the nutrition analyses were calculated using weights or measures for cooked meat.

- Garnishes and optional ingredients were not included in the nutrition analyses.
- If a marinade was brushed over a food during cooking, the analysis includes all of the marinade.
- When two ingredient options appear in a recipe, calculations were made using the first one.
- For ingredients of variable weight (such as "2½- to 3-pound broiler-fryer chicken") or for recipes with a serving range ("Makes 4 to 6 servings"), calculations were made using the first figure.

| | Per Serving | | | | | | Percent USRDA Per Serving | | | | | | | |
	Calories	Protein (g)	Carbohydrate (g)	Fat (g)	Sodium (mg)	Potassium (mg)	Protein	Vitamin A	Vitamin C	Thiamine	Riboflavin	Niacin	Calcium	Iron
Eggs and Cheese														
Beer-Cheese Soup (p. 44)	320	16	21	17	707	106	25	14	1	14	20	9	40	7
Broccoli Frittata (p. 60)	254	15	4	20	319	232	23	46	46	8	21	2	19	13
Easy Farmer's Breakfast (p. 63)	394	19	18	27	504	388	29	20	36	21	20	10	8	19
Ham and Potato Quiche (p. 95)	370	17	20	25	655	242	27	22	4	12	23	7	29	12
Hearty Italian Quiche (p. 92)	354	14	18	25	491	190	22	12	3	15	20	9	19	9
Pepperoni Frittata (p. 63)	457	20	11	37	1312	233	30	30	0	12	26	10	10	16
Quiche in Pasta Crust (p. 94)	384	21	26	21	455	223	33	18	1	23	27	12	40	13
Spaghetti Sauce Lasagna (p. 108)	359	22	33	15	847	137	34	14	2	19	24	9	30	11
Three-Cheese Quiche (p. 94)	387	16	21	27	481	183	25	14	1	12	24	5	29	8
Turkey Quiche (p. 95)	352	25	25	17	674	302	39	17	0	10	26	16	39	14
Zucchini Lasagna (p. 106)	323	18	29	15	273	375	27	28	36	22	22	14	31	10
Fish and Seafood														
Crunchy Tuna Salad (p. 16)	276	20	12	17	523	422	30	12	40	8	14	37	7	12
Fish Chowder (p. 42)	397	26	18	24	230	728	40	90	48	13	28	14	27	7
Fish with Cream Sauce (p. 68)	217	27	4	9	234	434	41	10	11	6	8	14	5	6
Italian-Style Fish (p. 68)	153	20	5	6	489	436	30	14	8	7	7	13	14	7
Monterey Fish Salad (p. 69)	313	22	11	21	379	717	34	15	26	9	11	12	21	10
No-Chop Shrimp Stir-Fry (p. 101)	366	24	38	13	1463	673	37	18	44	15	18	37	12	21
Orange-Poached Fish (p. 66)	312	21	53	1	246	858	33	162	63	25	8	21	12	16
Oven-Fried Fish (p. 51)	283	29	9	13	372	423	45	11	0	9	11	17	5	9
Salmon Potato Salad (p. 17)	553	32	36	32	1763	1275	49	15	60	15	23	57	30	22
Salmon Stroganoff Skillet (p. 36)	343	23	24	17	880	502	35	21	14	20	20	44	26	12
Scallops and Pea Pods (p. 98)	340	25	40	8	897	618	38	11	26	24	8	16	13	26
Seafood and Wild Rice Salad (p. 23)	330	21	33	13	1063	275	32	7	22	12	6	15	13	21
Seafood Louis (p. 14)	478	18	24	37	564	752	28	41	72	13	17	12	12	23
Shrimp Frittata (p. 62)	246	20	5	17	367	289	30	38	60	8	21	5	14	18

	Per Serving						Percent USRDA Per Serving						
	Calories	Protein (g)	Carbohydrate (g)	Fat (g)	Sodium (mg)	Potassium (mg)	Protein	Vitamin A	Vitamin C	Thiamine	Riboflavin	Niacin	Calcium	Iron

Fish and Seafood *(continued)*

	Calories	Protein (g)	Carbohydrate (g)	Fat (g)	Sodium (mg)	Potassium (mg)	Protein	Vitamin A	Vitamin C	Thiamine	Riboflavin	Niacin	Calcium	Iron
Shrimp in Cheddar Sauce (p. 83)	439	21	28	26	542	248	32	20	15	20	20	14	28	16
Tuna-Broccoli-Sauced Pastry (p. 22)	320	20	20	18	1018	352	31	23	45	12	15	38	9	11
Tuna-Spaghetti Skillet (p. 38)	449	25	34	24	1149	522	38	40	86	23	24	48	11	14
Wine-Sauced Fish Steaks (p. 69)	511	33	30	27	807	722	50	24	10	38	8	68	2	14

Meats

	Calories	Protein (g)	Carbohydrate (g)	Fat (g)	Sodium (mg)	Potassium (mg)	Protein	Vitamin A	Vitamin C	Thiamine	Riboflavin	Niacin	Calcium	Iron
Barbecue-Style Pork Roast (p. 54)	312	29	10	16	311	625	45	19	138	45	20	30	4	24
Barley-Sausage Skillet (p. 39)	469	21	28	31	1953	412	33	44	18	24	16	18	15	18
Biscuit-Topped Skillet (p. 75)	446	20	42	22	1359	477	31	23	12	16	26	24	15	24
Bratwurst-Potato Chowder (p. 44)	436	19	37	24	1256	862	30	56	32	20	33	18	28	14
Cheese and Pastrami Hoagies (p. 10)	420	19	33	23	849	176	30	13	7	15	19	12	23	15
Chili-Bean Dish (p. 75)	368	25	21	21	842	587	38	51	42	12	20	22	25	21
Corn-Bread-Coated Pork Chops (p. 50)	332	25	17	18	619	301	38	0	4	57	19	29	5	19
Corned Beef and Brussels Sprouts (p. 57)	483	27	24	31	968	698	42	6	106	12	17	17	4	23
Cranberry-Peach Ham (p. 83)	519	21	65	19	1262	482	32	92	24	38	13	25	4	21
Creamed Peas and Beef (p. 77)	556	21	36	36	1061	400	33	22	16	41	25	24	9	22
Dilled Meat and Potato Chowder (p. 76)	261	17	18	13	449	446	26	16	17	11	17	19	10	13
Easy Corned Beef Stroganoff (p. 25)	494	33	36	24	1235	303	50	16	13	31	32	35	11	33
Easy Reubens (p. 11)	512	23	32	33	1598	241	36	7	15	12	18	12	23	18
Family-Size Hero Sandwich (p. 8)	489	20	50	23	1241	465	31	14	43	24	13	16	8	17
German-Style Pot Roast (p. 57)	646	31	22	48	327	722	48	108	31	11	17	30	4	26
Ground Meat Freezer Base (p.72)	170	13	4	11	177	199	21	15	3	5	8	14	2	11
Ham and Apricot Kabobs (p. 88)	521	25	50	25	983	474	38	4	87	41	15	22	3	23
Ham and Macaroni Slaw (p. 17)	757	24	49	53	791	467	37	12	44	43	28	22	31	18
Ham and Pecan Stir-Fry (p. 102)	518	19	38	32	1413	427	29	4	95	42	13	19	4	21
Ham and Shrimp Creole (p. 20)	367	25	43	10	552	801	38	50	93	34	12	29	8	31
Ham and Spaetzle Skillet (p. 39)	473	23	39	25	1414	465	36	15	16	42	26	25	11	23
Hearty Open-Face Sandwiches (p. 73)	405	21	38	20	1137	440	32	23	11	13	19	19	13	19
Individual Ham Loaves (p. 31)	467	31	14	31	1173	417	47	13	14	61	22	26	6	26
Macaroni-Beef Supper (p. 37)	587	30	39	35	1438	459	45	14	9	22	25	34	10	28
Meat and Potato Kabobs (p. 88)	682	24	26	54	1904	739	36	1	51	12	16	27	5	25
Meaty Cream Cheese Stroganoff (p. 74)	454	22	26	29	301	314	33	32	5	14	25	22	9	17
Mexicali Skillet (p. 34)	347	15	36	16	549	485	23	25	45	15	13	13	18	18
Mexican Manicotti (p. 109)	647	29	50	37	2304	721	45	19	12	29	27	31	21	29
Mostaccioli with Italian Sauce (p. 82)	466	23	44	22	740	707	35	41	54	48	25	37	8	26
Mustard-Sauced Liver (p. 103)	357	24	20	20	844	376	36	811	42	16	189	65	2	40
Old-Fashioned Meat Loaf (p. 30)	336	24	14	20	541	398	38	10	7	11	17	24	7	20
Oriental Beef (p. 76)	420	25	33	20	1498	461	38	27	25	21	18	27	6	26
Oven Swiss Steak (p. 116)	302	23	10	19	253	415	36	11	21	8	13	25	2	18
Pizza Manicotti (p. 109)	494	28	42	23	952	275	43	7	5	23	20	27	22	22
Pizza-Style Meat Loaf (p. 28)	368	27	15	22	567	276	41	5	2	8	16	24	13	21
Saucy Orange Beef (p. 82)	372	21	40	13	1145	481	32	9	63	16	14	25	5	22
Sausage-Onion Stir-Fry (p. 103)	568	25	38	33	2553	627	38	1	77	32	19	29	6	27
Sausage-Vegetable Stew (p. 25)	509	19	36	32	1877	693	29	165	40	26	21	27	4	23
Savory Beef-Vegetable Soup (p. 45)	293	19	16	17	858	498	28	73	21	11	15	23	6	15
Skillet Stuffed Peppers (p. 74)	352	23	21	20	668	547	35	45	114	15	19	21	23	19

	Per Serving					Percent USRDA Per Serving							
	Calories	Protein (g)	Carbohydrate (g)	Fat (g)	Sodium (mg)	Potassium (mg)	Protein	Vitamin A	Vitamin C	Thiamine	Riboflavin	Niacin	Calcium	Iron

Meats *(continued)*

	Calories	Protein (g)	Carbohydrate (g)	Fat (g)	Sodium (mg)	Potassium (mg)	Protein	Vitamin A	Vitamin C	Thiamine	Riboflavin	Niacin	Calcium	Iron
Spicy Pork Kabobs (p. 89)	392	19	22	26	1035	486	29	4	29	32	16	20	5	20
Spinach and Lamb Loaf (p. 31)	374	25	10	26	374	444	38	80	23	14	25	22	17	15
Stew with Potato Topper (p. 80)	459	24	34	26	734	803	36	186	24	10	18	22	10	24
Stuffed Pita Pockets (p. 10)	309	16	15	20	397	304	25	13	16	7	12	10	23	10
Sweet-Sour Beef and Vegetable Salad (p. 77)	285	17	24	15	245	775	27	156	93	13	24	22	12	29
Teriyaki-Sauced Beef and Zucchini (p. 102)	340	21	27	16	1171	457	32	7	39	14	15	26	5	21
Veal Parmigiano (p. 51)	411	29	18	24	867	255	45	14	0	7	21	20	28	18
Zesty Pork Loaves (p. 30)	457	28	10	33	628	273	43	10	0	32	24	20	26	18

Poultry

	Calories	Protein (g)	Carbohydrate (g)	Fat (g)	Sodium (mg)	Potassium (mg)	Protein	Vitamin A	Vitamin C	Thiamine	Riboflavin	Niacin	Calcium	Iron
Chicken and Bulgur Skillet (p. 36)	336	25	39	10	485	494	39	43	87	14	15	40	7	16
Chicken and Corkscrew Macaroni (p. 23)	449	32	46	15	1368	362	50	39	52	35	29	42	24	19
Chicken and Fruit Salad (p. 16)	493	22	38	30	430	850	34	32	86	12	20	26	8	18
Chicken Lasagna (p. 108)	349	21	28	17	617	290	32	18	17	20	24	21	17	10
Chicken Liver Stir-Fry (p. 101)	381	29	35	12	286	338	44	215	115	33	145	63	4	49
Chicken-Mushroom Frittata (p. 62)	232	21	3	14	260	273	33	19	5	8	22	18	7	14
Cranberry-Orange Turkey Stir-Fry (p. 100)	342	34	37	8	1065	761	53	11	38	15	21	54	8	20
Deli Salad Sandwiches (p. 10)	465	16	37	29	537	327	25	5	11	22	13	18	7	14
Easy Chicken Stir-Fry (p. 100)	231	20	15	10	1044	248	31	30	91	8	18	36	5	12
Freezer-to-Table Skillet Supper (p. 37)	386	31	41	11	1500	649	47	172	19	29	27	43	8	29
Herbed Broccoli Soup (p. 45)	297	29	19	12	574	595	45	45	88	12	29	33	33	10
Italian Chicken Kabobs (p. 89)	403	32	8	27	839	408	49	4	50	12	37	75	3	14
Italian Seasoned Chicken Thighs (p. 50)	388	31	15	22	376	362	48	10	0	9	33	39	2	18
Lemon-Herbed Chicken (p. 112)	227	29	1	11	124	12	44	26	6	7	34	43	2	16
Oven-Fried Chicken (p. 48)	271	28	17	9	252	67	42	35	9	20	45	46	4	18
Potato Shell Turkey Pie (p. 22)	419	19	28	26	698	679	29	59	16	8	16	21	18	11
Rush Hour Simmer Dinner (p. 38)	413	30	37	16	847	354	46	137	22	33	19	42	5	19
Sweet 'n' Sour Chicken Dinner (p. 56)	381	31	56	4	534	473	48	164	79	20	18	61	8	22
Teriyaki Chicken Kabobs (p. 86)	335	31	11	17	1347	331	48	30	77	8	18	58	6	16
Turkey Club Sandwiches (p. 11)	505	35	67	12	746	736	53	8	11	22	24	41	31	20
Turkey Roast with Sweet Potatoes (p. 56)	459	32	39	19	109	698	49	153	31	12	19	33	5	19

Miscellaneous

	Calories	Protein (g)	Carbohydrate (g)	Fat (g)	Sodium (mg)	Potassium (mg)	Protein	Vitamin A	Vitamin C	Thiamine	Riboflavin	Niacin	Calcium	Iron
Baked Squash with Peas (p. 115)	114	5	27		246	772	7	50	57	13	14	9	6	11
Deep-Dish Apple Pie (p. 115)	345	2	55	14	234	135	3	4	3	9	5	5	1	7
Peach Crisp (p. 116)	424	4	64	19	148	294	7	24	76	10	6	7	4	12